So, You Think
You Know Boston?

People, Places, Folklore, Trivia
and Treasures

Henry M. Quinlan
Theresa Driscoll

Omni Publishing Co.
2024

Published by Omni Publishing Co.
www.omni-pub.com

Cover Design: Dave Derby
www.DerbyCreative.com

Library of Congress cataloging in publication data

Quinlan, Henry M.
Driscoll, Theresa

So, You Think You Know the Boston?
People, Places, Folklore, Trivia and Treasures

ISBN: 978-1-928758-15-0

Introduction

Imagine exploring Boston beyond the usual tourist attractions, uncovering hidden gems and experiencing the city like a true local. With "So, You Think You Know Boston?" your adventure begins here. This captivating book takes you on a vivid tour through the city's diverse neighborhoods, offering brief yet enriching descriptions that bring each area to life.

Unearth Hidden Gems: From the Mapparium at the Christian Science headquarters, to Brook Farm in West Roxbury and the Tea Room in the Back Bay, "So, You Think You Know Boston?" goes beyond the surface, revealing the lesser-known treasures that make this city unique. Whether it's a quiet garden in the Fenway or The East Boston Greenway, you'll discover places that even long-time Bostonians might have missed.

Perfect for Locals and Visitors Alike: This book isn't just for tourists – every Bostonian will find something new and exciting within its pages. Rediscover your city with fresh eyes, armed with insider knowledge and fascinating tidbits that enrich your daily experiences. Impress your friends with your newfound expertise on Boston's hidden corners and forgotten stories.

Your Ultimate City Companion: "So, You Think You Know Boston?" isn't merely a guidebook; it's your personal companion to the city's soul. Its narrative style and engaging storytelling captivate readers, making it a delightful read whether you're planning your next outing or simply indulging in some armchair travel.

Don't miss out on the adventure that awaits within Boston's city limits. Grab your copy of "So, You Think You Know Boston?" today and start exploring the city like never before.

Henry Quinlan and Theresa Driscoll, co-authors, have over 100 years of combined experience in the City of Boston. This book reflects their knowledge and love of the City.

Authors Information

Henry M. Quinlan is the publisher of Omni Publishing Company. He is the author in three other books in the series, other *books in the series include "So You Think You Know the South Coast?," "So You Think You Know Cape Cod?,"* and *"So, You Think You Know Tennis?."*

And the newly released *"Secret, Hidden and Forgotten Cape Cod."*

He also is a lecturer for senior citizen groups. His talks are: "Happiness for Seniors – What It is and How to Obtain It," "How to Write and Self-Publish Your Story," "How to Build Your Emotional Pension," and "The Ukraine War and Vladimir Putin."

Theresa Driscoll is a freelance writer and editor with years of experience in the publishing industry and as a communication professional for non-profits. Theresa is a graduate of Boston Latin School and the University of Massachusetts at Amherst. A lifelong resident of Boston, she lives with her family in West Roxbury and spends her free time finding new gems to explore in Boston's neighborhoods.

Table of Contents

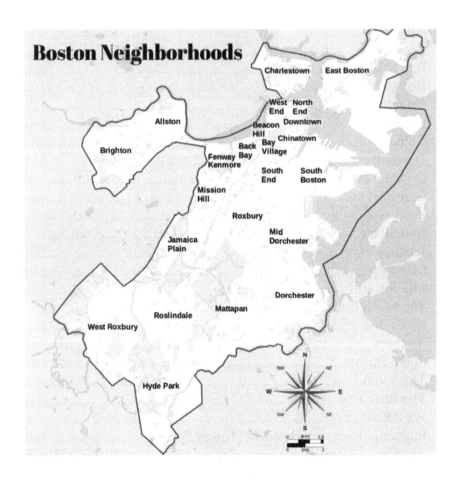

Boston Neighborhoods

Allston

Allston is a vibrant neighborhood with an urban vibe, whose history is deeply intertwined with Boston's growth and development. Originally inhabited by Native American tribes and settled by European colonists in the 17th century, Allston evolved as a rural farming community. The construction of railroads in the mid-1800s facilitated the growth of Allston as an accessible suburb of Boston, attracting industrial and residential development.

By the turn of the 20th century, Allston's urbanization was well under way, driven by newly arrived immigrants looking for work in nearby industries. The neighborhood's landscape transformed as single-family homes were converted into multi-unit residences to meet housing demand. Its proximity to universities, especially Harvard University and Boston University, shaped its identity as a hub for academics, artists, musicians and students.

Over the decades, Allston has experienced waves of gentrification and development. The construction of the Massachusetts Turnpike and the expansion of nearby educational institutions led to changes in the neighborhood's demographics and landscape. While some historic buildings have been preserved, modern structures have replaced others.

Allston has undergone significant revitalization efforts and urban planning initiatives in recent years, aimed at enhancing public spaces, promoting sustainable transportation options, and preserving the area's cultural heritage. The transformation of the Boston Landing development into a mixed-use space featuring offices, retail establishments, sports facilities and public transportation hubs has further impacted Allston's evolution.

Today, Allston is known for its diverse population, cultural vibrancy, and eclectic mix of restaurants, cafes, and shops. The neighborhood's proximity to prominent universities continues to attract students and academics, maintaining its reputation as an intellectual and artistic hub. Its history as a farming community, an industrial suburb, a haven for artists, and a center of activism has shaped Allston into the multifaceted and dynamic neighborhood it is today.

Do You Know Allston?

Originally known as Little Cambridge, this neighborhood was named after American painter and poet **Washington Allston** in the mid-19th century. Born in South Carolina, Allston attended Harvard University and spent nearly 20 years painting and writing poetry in Europe before resettling in Cambridge after his wife's death. Allston was the first important influencer of American landscape painting known for "The Deluge" (1804) and "Elijah in the Desert" (1818). His painting **"The Fields of West Boston"** is said to have inspired the Allston name.

The eastern part of Brighton, now known as Allston, was the site of a new railroad depot in 1867 developed around **the railroad and livestock industries**, with significant stockyards in the northern part of Brighton.

By the early 20th century, Allston had become a bustling area with a mix of residential and commercial properties, including Boston's first **"Automile"** along Commonwealth Avenue, lined with automobile dealerships and related businesses.

While Harvard University is primarily located in neighboring Cambridge, Allston is home to **Harvard Stadium**, used for football, lacrosse, and other events. The stadium, built in 1903, is one of the oldest college football stadiums in the country.

Allston has a lively music scene, with numerous venues hosting live performances by local and touring bands. The **Brighton Music Hall** is a popular spot for concerts, offering a diverse range of musical genres and fostering a sense of community among music enthusiasts.

Harvard University owns substantial land in the area and has undertaken major building projects, including the **Paulson School of Engineering and Applied Sciences** and the **Enterprise Research Campus.** This expansion has brought new residential units, commercial spaces and amenities, contributing to Allston's dynamic character.

WGBH, which stands for Great Blue Hill (the location of its original transmitter), began as an FM radio station before expanding into television broadcasting. In 1964, WGBH moved its main studios to a facility on Western Avenue in Allston, adjacent to Brighton. WGBH again relocated to Market Street in Brighton in 2007.

Braves Field, now Boston University's Nickerson Field, made history in 1929 when it hosted the first Sunday baseball games ever played in Boston. This was significant as city blue laws had previously prohibited professional sports on Sundays.

In 1935, Braves Field became the backdrop for **Babe Ruth's final season** in Major League Baseball. Hoping for a chance to manage the team, the legendary slugger joined the Boston Braves after his illustrious career with the New York Yankees. Ruth's tenure with the Braves was brief but provided fans at opportunity to witness his final at-bats.

The **City Series** between the Boston Braves and the Boston Red Sox was an annual exhibition series played before the official start of the regular season beginning in 1901. The series ended in 1952 when the Braves moved to Milwaukee.

On October 19, 1963, **President John F. Kennedy** made his last public appearance in Massachusetts before his assassination on November 22, 1963. In a rare photo, President Kennedy was pictured smoking a cigar at a fundraising dinner at the **Commonwealth Armory.** As the headquarters for the Massachusetts Army National Guard, the Armory hosted various military units and activities from its construction in 1914-

1915 until its departure in December 1988. Demolished in 2002, the Armory site is now occupied by the Agganis Arena.

Boston University's growth has shaped many areas of Allston. In 1920, BU purchased 15 acres of land between Commonwealth Avenue and the Charles River to unify its previously scattered schools and colleges, creating what is now known as the Charles River Campus. During his long tenure (1926-1951) **BU President Daniel Marsh** incorporated Sargent College into BU, founded the School of Social Work, the School of Nursing, the School of Public Relations and the General College.

The rock band **Aerosmith** lived at 1325 Commonwealth Avenue between 1970 and 1972. There's a historic plaque on the building commemorating their time there.

The Boston Celtics and New Balance Athletics opened the **Auerbach Center at Allston's Boston Landing** as the team's official practice facility. The 70,000 square foot structure, which houses two full sized NBA basketball courts with parquet floors and state-of-the-art practice and recovery equipment, honors the late Red Auerbach, who led the Celtics to nine NBA championships.

Braves Field in the 1940s.

10

Back Bay

The Back Bay is a neighborhood built on reclaimed land in the Charles River basin. Construction began in 1859 as the demand for luxury housing in the city exceeded availability - and the area was entirely built by around 1900. It is most famous for its rows of Victorian brownstone homes – considered one of the best-preserved examples of 19th-century urban design in the U.S. – as well as numerous architecturally significant buildings and cultural institutions, such as the Boston Public Library and Boston Architectural College.

Back Bay was originally a small saltwater bay on the shore of the Shawmut Peninsula and the Boston Neck, on which the City of Boston was built. By the 1800s, the success of Boston's shipping and manufacturing industries had led to intense overcrowding in the city and Back Bay was seen as a prime location for expansion. In 1820, the Commonwealth of Massachusetts chartered the Boston and Roxbury Mill Corporation and approved a long mill dam (under present-day Beacon Street) to cut off 430 acres of tidal flats from the river, serving as a toll road to Watertown. The mill dam created a stagnant body of water, quickly polluted by industrial waste and sewage, turning Back Bay into a fetid swamp.

In 1856, the Massachusetts legislature approved a plan to fill in Back Bay and create a new neighborhood. The project was overseen by the Back Bay Development Company, headed by Alexander Hamilton Rice, a wealthy businessman who envisioned Back Bay as a fashionable residential district. He hired Frederick Law Olmsted, the landscape architect who designed Central Park in New York City, to create the park system

11

for Back Bay. Filling in Back Bay was a massive undertaking. More than 450 acres of land were filled with trash and mud from the flats of the South Bay, and sand and gravel brought in by railroad from Needham, a town west of the city. The fill was dumped into the bay and compacted by steam-powered rollers. The streets were laid out in a grid pattern, and the blocks were divided into 25-foot-wide lots.

Construction of the Back Bay began in 1859, and the first houses were completed in 1861. The neighborhood quickly became popular with Boston's wealthy residents, attracted to its spacious homes, tree-lined streets, and proximity to the Public Garden. By the 1880s, Back Bay was one of the most fashionable neighborhoods in Boston. The Back Bay continued to grow and develop in the late 19th and early 20th centuries. Many of the city's cultural institutions were built in Back Bay during this time, including the Boston Public Library (1895), the Museum of Fine Arts (1876), and the Boston Symphony Hall (1900). Back Bay also became a center for the arts and entertainment, with theaters, opera houses, and concert halls.

The Back Bay is still one of the most desirable neighborhoods in Boston. Today, it is home to a mix of wealthy families, professionals, and students. The neighborhood is also a popular tourist destination, thanks to its beautiful architecture, tree-lined streets, and proximity to many of Boston's most popular attractions.

Do You Know Back Bay?

The **Commonwealth Avenue Mall** is a 32-acre "grand allée" of shade trees designed in the French boulevard style by American architect Arthur Gilman between 1856 and 1888. It connects the Public Garden to the Back Bay Fens and features a mixture of large-scale shade trees, along with statues, benches, and walkways. Initially planted with American and European elms, the Mall's tree planting patterns were later influenced by Frederick Law Olmsted and Charles Sprague Sargent. The

Mall is known for its elegant residential architecture and serves as a crucial green link in Boston's "Emerald Necklace." Preserved and enhanced by the Friends of the Public Garden since 1970, it is listed on the National Register of Historic Places.

In 1986, the National Park Service designated the **Boston Public Library's McKim Building** a National Historic Landmark, citing it as "the first outstanding example of "Renaissance Beaux-Arts Classicism in America." The library offers free tours to the public to view the exquisite murals series by John Singer Sargent, Edwin Austin Abbey, and Pierre Puvis de Chavannes, and to view the peaceful inner courtyard and additional works of famed sculptors and painters. **Bates Hall**, the iconic reading room located on the second floor of the McKim building, is named for Joshua Bates, a London merchant banker born in Weymouth who in 1852 donated $50,000 for the library's establishment and another $50,000 to purchase books. He was the first major benefactor of the BPL and initiated that its services be "free to all."

The **Boston Public Library** at Copley Square is known by most, but the afternoon tea parties hosted there are a delightful surprise to many. From Monday to Saturday between 11:30 and 3:30 pm, you can sip tea and eat petit fours at the Library's Courtyard.

The Boston Marathon's finish line is outside the front doors of the BPL. The annual marathon is the world's oldest marathon. From just 15 participants in 1897, it now attracts about 30,000 registered participants annually. Beloved Boston Marathon figures include: Johnny Kelly, who ran 61 Boston Marathons, and won two; the Hoyt father-son team who ran 32 marathons, with Dick pushing Rick's wheelchair; and the most famous four-legged supporter, Spencer the golden retriever who lifted spirits year after year near the Ashland starting line.

The **Boston Marathon Bombing** occurred on Patriots' Day in 2013, on Boylston Street near the finish line of the Boston Marathon. The two bombs detonated just 12 seconds apart. In addition to three direct fatalities, over 260 people were injured in the attack, with 17 people losing limbs. The manhunt for the suspects led to an unprecedented shutdown of much of the Greater Boston area, with residents asked to stay in their homes and businesses told not to open.

The **Boston Common** is the oldest public park in the U.S., established in 1634. Its 50 acre span has served various purposes over the centuries, including grazing livestock, military training, and even public executions. Today, its vibrant green space features ballfields, the Frog Pond, ice skating rink and numerous monuments. Historically significant events, including anti-slavery meetings, Civil War recruitment, and speeches by figures like Martin Luther King Jr., have taken place here.

The Boston Public Garden is a 24-acre botanical garden located in the heart of Boston, adjacent to the historic Boston Common. It was established in 1837, making it the first public botanical garden in America. The garden features winding paths, vibrant floral displays, and a picturesque lagoon where the iconic Swan Boats offer leisurely, pedal-powered rides. Victorian-era statues and fountains adorn the landscape, including the famous George Washington statue.

One of the most unique mansions in Back Bay is the **Ayer Mansion**, the only surviving residential property fully designed by Louis Comfort Tiffany, famous for his stained-glass work. The Commonwealth Avenue mansion features Tiffany's distinctive mosaic tiles and curved lines.

Bodega, a secret retail venue, is concealed behind a seemingly ordinary convenience store on Clearway Street. To visit, find and open a hidden door disguised as an obsolete Snapple vending machine.

There is another **Make Way for Ducklings** statue in Moscow, Russia. It was given to the children of Moscow by President HW Bush and Mrs. Bush as part of a Summit in 1990. Both sets of ducks were created by Nancy Schron, noted sculptress.

The Mapparium is a three-story-tall, inside-out stained glass globe that visitors can walk through on a glass bridge. *More on page 131.*

According to the US census, 86 percent of Back Bay residents over the age of 25 have completed at least a **bachelor's degree**, nearly double the average for Boston.

Bay Village

Bay Village is the smallest officially recognized neighborhood in Boston, covering approximately 12 square blocks. Home to 1,300 residents living primarily in Federal and Greek Revival influenced brick row houses, the neighborhood is one of the city's most undiscovered neighborhoods and is nicknamed "Boston's Secret Garden."

Originally known as the Church Street District, Bay Village was developed in the 1820s on land that had been mudflats. The area underwent significant engineering work to raise its elevation, addressing sewage issues caused by nearby developments in the South End and Back Bay. This project involved raising 457 houses and numerous other structures by 12 feet, a massive undertaking that took about two years to complete. In the early 20th century, Bay Village became a hub for Boston's film industry, earning the nickname "Hollywood East." Notable historical events include the tragic Cocoanut Grove nightclub fire in 1942, which resulted in significant loss of life and remains one of the deadliest fires in U.S. history.

Bay Village is characterized by its narrow, one-way streets and quiet atmosphere, making it pedestrian-friendly. The neighborhood features brick sidewalks and gas streetlamps, contributing to its historic charm. The Bay Village Historic District was designated in 1983, protecting the architectural integrity of the area and ensuring that any exterior changes to buildings undergo review by the Bay Village Historic District Commission. Bay Village borders Chinatown,, Back Bay, the South End and Downtown, so residents are within walking distance to many key areas, including the Theatre District, Boston Common, and the Public Garden.

This proximity provides residents with easy access to cultural events, restaurants, and entertainment options.

Do You Know Bay Village?

The **Federal Townhouses,** preserved red brick townhouses, located on Fayette and Melrose Street date back to the 19th century

Our Lady of Victories Church established by the Marist Fathers in 1880, features 14 large German-designed stained glass windows, with some windows originating from Chartres, France. It serves as a French National Church, although services are conducted in English.

The **Art Deco** warehouses that were once part of the neighborhood's film industry have been converted into luxury condos. They showcase the Art Deco architectural style that was popular in the early 20th century.

The Castle, built in the 1890s at 130 Columbus Avenue, originally housed the First Corps of Cadets and is a prominent example of the neighborhood's historic architecture. The Castle faithfully emulates medieval design, despite being built during the late Victorian period. It features a six-story crenellated tower with slit windows, a drawbridge, corbel towers and rustic granite blocks. Now officially "The Saunders Castle at Park Plaza," owned by the Park Plaza Hotel, the Castle hosts special events, conferences, trade shows, and exhibits.

Bay Village boasts an impressive **Walk Score of 98**, making it one of the most walkable neighborhoods in Boston. The area is designed for pedestrians, with brick-paved sidewalks and minimal vehicle traffic, allowing visitors to explore comfortably. Walking tours are available that delve into the neighborhood's past, including its transformation from a hub of artisans to a center for the New England film industry in the early 20th century

Beacon Hill

Beacon Hill is one of Boston's most historic and iconic neighbor-hoods, known for its rich history and distinctive architecture, and characterized by its narrow, gaslit streets and brick sidewalks. The origins and development of Beacon Hill reflect the broader historical and social changes in Boston from the 17th century to the present day.

Beacon Hill's history dates back to the early 17th century when it was originally known as Tri-mountain or Tremont due to its three prominent peaks. The area was also referred to as Sentry Hill after English settlers erected a wooden beacon atop the hill in 1635 to warn of potential dangers or attacks. This beacon gave the hill its enduring name, Beacon Hill. The first European settler on Beacon Hill was William Blaxton, who built a house and orchard on the south slope in 1625. By 1630, the Massachusetts Bay Company had settled Boston, and the southwestern slope of Beacon Hill was used for military drills and livestock grazing. The area became known for its strategic importance and scenic views, which later attracted wealthy residents.

In the late 18th century, Beacon Hill began to transform from a rural area into a more developed neighborhood. Charles Bulfinch, a prominent architect, played a crucial role in this transformation. In 1787, he designed the Massachusetts State House, which became a central landmark of the neighborhood when completed in 1795. Bulfinch also collaborated with the Mount Vernon Proprietors to develop the area west of the State House into a residential district for Boston's elite. The construction of grand mansions and Federal-style rowhouses characterized the early development of Beacon Hill. Notable families, such as the Hancocks and

17

the Lowells, built opulent homes in the area, establishing Beacon Hill as a prestigious address. The neighborhood's narrow, gaslit streets and brick sidewalks added to its charm and exclusivity.

Throughout the 19th century, Beacon Hill continued to evolve. The neighborhood saw an influx of Irish, Jewish, and other immigrants, leading to the construction of brick apartment buildings and tenements. Despite these changes, Beacon Hill remained a desirable and affluent area. The late 19th and early 20th centuries brought further development and preservation efforts. The Beacon Hill Historic District was established in 1955 to protect the neighborhood's architectural heritage. The district was expanded several times, and the Beacon Hill Architectural Commission was created to oversee exterior alterations and maintain the area's historic character.

Today, Beacon Hill is one of Boston's most sought-after neighborhoods, known for its historic charm and vibrant community. The area is home to a mix of wealthy residents, professionals, and families. The Massachusetts State House remains a central feature, symbolizing the neighborhood's historical and political significance. Beacon Hill's narrow streets, lined with Federal and Greek Revival-style homes, continue to attract visitors and residents alike. The neighborhood's rich history is commemorated through various landmarks and institutions, such as the Black Heritage Trail and the Museum of African American History, which highlight the contributions of African American residents and the area's role in the abolitionist movement. In addition to its historical significance, Beacon Hill offers many modern amenities, boutique shops, restaurants and parks, and the neighborhood's blend of historic preservation and contemporary living makes it a unique and desirable place to live in Boston. Beacon Hill's origins as a strategic lookout point and its development into a prestigious residential area reflect the broader historical and social changes in Boston. Today, it remains a vibrant and historically rich neighborhood, cherished for its architectural beauty and cultural significance.

Do You Know Beacon Hill?

Many of the row houses on Beacon Hill were designed by famous architects like **Charles Bulfinch** in the Federal and Greek Revival styles.

The **Mount Vernon Proprietors**, an early land development company, purchased land west of the State House for residential development in the early 19th century.

By the late 19th century, brick apartment buildings and tenements were constructed on the backside of Beacon Hill to accommodate an influx of immigrants to the area.

The **State House** is open to the public, with tours available weekdays between 10 am and 3:30 pm. There are two statues on the State House grounds you should make a point of seeing. One is a statue of **Anne Hutchinson**, who was driven out of Boston in 1638 for not conforming to Puritanism. The other is a statue of John F. Kennedy, which was a gift from the people of Massachusetts.

Acorn Street is one of the most photographed streets in Boston, with its narrow road lined by brick rowhouses.

Charles Street, at the bottom of Beacon Hill and dating from the 19th century, is the main shopping and dining street in Beacon Hill. The street is the start and finish point for the annual Boston Athletic Association 10K race, which began in 2011. Trivia experts will tell you that Edgar Allan Poe was born at 62 Carver Street, since renamed Charles Street South. Another interesting tidbit is that part of Martin Scorsese's 2006 film *The Departed* was filmed on Charles Street.

The **Charles Street Meeting House** is an early-nineteenth-century historic church located at 70 Charles Street. Several Christian denominations, including Baptists, the First African Methodist Episcopal Church, and Unitarian Universalist, have called the church home. It was renovated in the 1980s – restoring and preserving the exterior – and adapted for use as office space. This project received awards from the National Trust for Historic Preservation and the American Institute of

Architects. The meeting house is a site on the **National Park Service's Black Heritage Trail** and is part of the Beacon Hill Historic District, listed on the National Register of Historic Places.

The **Nichols House Museum**, an 1805 row house renovated in 1830, showcases the lifestyle of the 19th century upper class.

Louisburg Square has always been THE place to live in Boston, and a number of recognizable names have made their home here. Charles Bulfinch, architect of the nearby State House lived here as well as John Singleton Copley, a famous American painter. Author Louisa May Alcott – of Little Women fame – made her home at number 10 and died there as well. Some say that opera singer Jenny Lind married here in the 1850s. More recent residents include Jack Welch and former U.S. Senator and presidential hopeful, John Kerry. The well-tended and pristine square itself is owned by the people who live in the surrounding homes. A symbol of exclusivity, the small, fenced park is the last private square in the city of Boston.

The Boston Athenaeum, founded in 1807, is one of the oldest libraries in the U.S. and houses impressive collections. It is a unique combination of library, museum, and cultural center in a magnificent landmark building. It is an independent library, with a circulating collection of over half a million books from works published in the 1800s to the latest best sellers. Special collections include active research holdings of 100,000 rare books, maps, and manuscripts, and 100,000 works of art, from paintings and sculpture to prints and photographs. Members, visitors, and the community enjoy a year-round schedule of cultural programming – author talks, book clubs, exhibitions, concerts, social gatherings, and opportunities for connection.

The North Slope area of Beacon Hill has deep ties to Boston's Black community and the abolitionist movement. During the 19th century, many famous Black and white abolitionists resided there, and the neighborhood was an important stop on the **Underground Railroad**. There are houses that were used to hide formerly enslaved people fleeing to Canada.

Brighton

Before the American Revolutionary War, Little Cambridge was a small, prosperous farming community with fewer than 300 residents. Its inhabitants included wealthy Boston merchants such as Benjamin Faneuil (after whom a street in Brighton is named). A key event in the history of Allston–Brighton was the establishment in 1775 of a cattle market to supply the Continental Army. Jonathan Winship I and Jonathan Winship II established the market, and in the post-war period that followed, the Winships became the largest meat packers in Massachusetts. The residents of Little Cambridge resolved to secede from Cambridge when the government made decisions detrimental to the cattle industry and failed to repair the Great Bridge linking Little Cambridge with Cambridge proper. Legislative approval for separation was obtained in 1807, and Little Cambridge renamed itself Brighton.

In 1820, the horticulture industry was introduced to the town. Over the next 20 years, Brighton blossomed as one of the most important gardening neighborhoods in the Boston area. Its businessmen did not neglect the cattle industry, however. In 1834, the Boston & Worcester Railroad was built, solidifying the community's hold on the cattle trade. By 1866, the town contained 41 slaughterhouses, which later were consolidated into the Brighton Stock Yards and Brighton Abattoir.

In October 1873, the Town of Brighton in Middlesex County voted to annex itself to the City of Boston in Suffolk County, and in January 1874 Brighton officially became part of the City of Boston.

The early 20th century brought waves of immigration, particularly from Ireland and Eastern Europe, further enriching Brighton's cultural fabric. The district's diversity was reflected in its architecture, local businesses, and places of worship. Brighton experienced economic prosperity and challenges from the Great Depression and World Wars.

In the mid-20th century, urban renewal efforts led to the construction of the Massachusetts Turnpike, reshaping the neighborhood's landscape and transportation network and altering the physical character of the area.

Today, Brighton is a thriving neighborhood of nearly 44,000 residents that showcases a blend of historical landmarks and modern amenities. Historic churches, landmarks like the Brighton Music Hall, and green spaces like the Chestnut Hill Reservoir contribute to the area's unique identity. Boston College also calls Brighton home, adding an academic dimension to the neighborhood's vibrancy.

Do You Know Brighton?

The area that would become Brighton was initially part of Cambridge (1630) and known as "**Little Cambridge.**" It is named after the English city of Brighton.

The Cattle Fair Hotel, with its hundred rooms, grand ballroom, and giant dining room, was the largest hotel in the Boston suburbs. The Cattle Fair Hotel Corporation also laid out the system of yards behind the hotel, the Brighton Stockyards, that long served as the principal headquarters of New England's cattle industry. The cattle sales in the ten years ending in 1845 averaged an enormous $2 million a year.

Saint John's Hall, the original building of St. John's Seminary on Lake Street, was built in 1884. The seminary building is home to a Romanesque chapel, administrative offices, classrooms, a refectory, and residences for priests and seminarians.

The **Cardinal's Residence** originally located on the grounds of St. John's Seminary is a three-story, ornate and opulent Italian Renaissance-style palazzo, financed to a large degree from a bequest from the family of Benjamin F. Keith, a vaudeville magnate. It was the centerpiece of the Archdiocese's "Little Rome" until it was sold to Boston College in 2004 to raise funds to pay the legal costs associated with sexual abuse scandal.

In the 1940s there were two reservoirs adjacent to Cleveland Circle. The one closest to Boston College was filled in and the land was sold to Boston College. Today the football stadium sits on the former reservoir. The remaining reservoir is the **Chestnut Hill Reservoir**, which was built in 1870 and provided drinking water to Boston until 1978.

The introduction of **electric streetcars** to Brighton in 1889 revolutionized transportation in the area and spurred significant urban development. This new mode of transport replaced horse-drawn carriages and made commuting to downtown Boston much faster and more convenient.

The **Brighton Cattle Market,** established in 1775, grew to be the largest in New England. Farmers and traders from across the region would bring their livestock to Brighton for sale and slaughter. **The Stockyard Restaurant** on Market Street is located in the area where the actual stockyards existed.

Oak Square, a section of Brighton, saw significant development in the late 19th century. Named after a large oak tree that once stood at its center, the square became a focal point for community life. The arrival of streetcar lines in the area spurred residential growth, with many of the Victorian-era homes that characterize the neighborhood built during this period.

St. Elizabeth's Hospital was founded in 1868 by five Catholic sisters from the Third Order of St. Francis. Initially located in Boston's North End, the hospital moved to Brighton in 1911, where it significantly expanded its facilities and services. The hospital's relocation brought advanced medical care to the area and became a major employer. Over the decades, St. Elizabeth's grew into a prominent medical institution. It played a crucial role in community health, particularly during times of crisis such as the 1918 influenza pandemic.

Boston Landing, marked a significant transformation of the neighborhood's landscape and economy. Anchored by the new world headquarters of **New Balance**, the complex includes office and retail space, a sports complex, and a commuter rail station. The development revitalized a former industrial area along the Massachusetts Turnpike, bringing new jobs and amenities. The inclusion of the Boston Bruins' practice facility and the Boston Celtics' training center added a major sports presence to the neighborhood. The Boston Landing commuter rail station, opened in 2017, significantly improved public transportation access in the area.

WGBH, Boston's public broadcasting station, has its headquarters on Guest Street in Brighton.

The **Brighton-Allston Heritage Museum** is located in the historic Veronica Smith building and showcases the history of the Brighton-Allston community.

The **Cleveland Circle Reservoir** is known for its 1.6-mile loop trail. Generally considered an easy route, it takes an average of 30 minutes to complete. This is a popular trail for birding, hiking, and running, but you can still enjoy some solitude during quieter times of day. The trail is open year-round.

Roger Baldwin of Brighton was one of the founders of the **ACLU**. He wanted its focus to be direct action and public education. Many of the ACLU's original landmark cases took place under his direction, including the Scopes Trial, the Sacco and Vanzetti murder trial, and its challenge to the ban on James Joyce's *Ulysses*.

Brighton Congregational Church, at 404 Washington Street, was built in 1921 to replace an earlier 1866 edifice that burned down. Designed by prominent theater architect Clarence Blackall, the church features excellent acoustics influenced by acoustical engineer Wallace Sabine. Blackall was known for designing many of Boston's theaters, including the Wang Center and Colonial Theater. The church's design reflects Blackall's theatrical expertise, particularly in its acoustic properties. It stands as a significant architectural landmark in Brighton Center, showcasing early 20th century ecclesiastical design.

The intersection of Beacon Street and Chestnut Hill Avenue near the Reservoir was named **Cleveland Circle** in 1908, shortly after the death of former U.S. President Grover Cleveland. The area's transformation from farmland to a desirable residential neighborhood was rapid. In 1889, the *Brighton Item* described the southeastern corner of Brighton as "vast acres of high, gravel land which have never produced anything for their owners but grass and tax bills." By 1890, it was being promoted as an idyllic neighborhood with magnificent views, perfect for residential development.

During **World War II** the US Army established an encampment on the Cleveland Circle Playground. The soldiers living there were guarding the reservoirs.

A photo of the BC Campus in the 1930s and the "second" reservoir in Brighton, now the football stadium.

25

The Bunker Hill Monument stretches high above Charlestown rooftops. Photo Credit: Leon Bredella on Unsplash

Charlestown

Charlestown is the city's oldest neighborhood, founded in 1629. Originally known as Mishawum, it sits on a peninsula bordered by the Charles River, Mystic River, and Boston Harbor. This historic area played a crucial role in American history, notably as the site of the Battle of Bunker Hill on June 17, 1775, during the Revolutionary War. The battle resulted in significant destruction, leading to a long period of rebuilding, with the Bunker Hill Monument erected between 1827 and 1843 to commemorate the event.

Charlestown was initially a separate town and served as the first capital of the Massachusetts Bay Colony. It became a city in 1848 and was annexed by Boston in 1874. The neighborhood has a rich Irish-American heritage, particularly after the influx of Irish immigrants during the Great Famine in the 1840s. This demographic shift established Charlestown as a center for Irish culture and Catholicism in Boston, a status it maintained well into the 20th century.

Today, Charlestown is known as a vibrant neighborhood featuring a charming combination of historic architecture – think original brick row houses – and modern waterfront condos. Local shops and restaurants mesh alongside historical sites including the Charlestown Navy Yard and the USS Constitution, the oldest commissioned warship still afloat. Charlestown has undergone significant gentrification to be what it is today, and continues to attract a diverse mix of residents, including young professionals and families.

Do You Know Charlestown?

The Freedom Trail, Boston's 2.5-mile walking route that connects 16 historically significant sites throughout the city, passes through Charlestown exploring sites related to Boston's role in the American Revolution. Charlestown sites include the Bunker Hill Monument and the USS Constitution.

The Bunker Hill Monument is a 221-foot granite obelisk commemorating the Battle of Bunker Hill, one of the most important battles of the American Revolutionary War. Built between 1825 and 1843, visitors can climb 294 steps to reach the summit and be rewarded with panoramic views of Boston. The monument is part of the Boston National Historical Park and is free to enter.

Established in 1801, the **Charlestown Navy Yard** is one of the oldest facilities in the U.S. Navy and offers a glimpse into America's maritime history. Now part of the Boston National Historical Park, it features the USS Constitution and a museum dedicated to its history. The Navy Yard's **USS Constitution Museum** is located in a renovated shipyard building and features interactive exhibits that tell the story of the USS Constitution and the people who built and sailed her.

The **USS Constitution**, known as "Old Ironsides," is a 1797 warship and the oldest commissioned naval vessel still afloat. The ship earned its nickname during the War of 1812 when British cannonballs appeared to bounce off the ship's wooden hull. Visitors may board and tour the ship free of charge. Each Fourth of July, the ship sets sail from its dock in the Navy Yard for its annual turnaround in Boston Harbor and a 21-gun salute at South Boston's Castle Island.

Paul Revere Park is a five-acre park along the Charles River and the Freedom Trail offering open space and walking and running paths. Views of the Charles River and the Zakim Bridge make it a unique spot for photo opportunities. The park features a large green lawn, an informal performance area, and a modern playground.

Winthrop Square, also known as the Training Field, is a historic park and former training field. Established in 1632 to train or drill bands of militia known as Training Bands, men from Charlestown drilled there prior to leaving to fight in the Civil War. The Charlestown Civil War Memorial is installed in the park.

Bunker Hill Catholic Cemetery, located behind St. Francis De-Sales Church on Bunker Hill Street, is one of a dozen memorials honoring the Irish Famine. Bishop Benedict Fenwick prevailed against resistance from local selectmen to open the cemetery in May 1832. The cemetery is the final resting places for thousands of Irish immigrants who came to Boston in the 19th century.

Courageous Sailing, a community sailing program located in the Navy Yard, focuses on providing accessible sailing experiences to a diverse community, particularly youth. Its youth programs aim to build leadership skills and confidence among children through hands-on sailing experiences and teamwork. Adult lessons, for all skill levels, and boat rentals are also available.

Dating back to 1780, the **Warren Tavern** opened in 1780 and claims to be the oldest bar in Massachusetts. Named in honor of Dr. Joseph Warren, a patriot who perished in the Battle of Bunker Hill, it was frequented by notable figures such as Paul Revere and George Washington. The Warren Tavern is a local favorite and a destination for tourists who wish to dine and socialize where many of our founding fathers gathered.

Car theft has a long history in Charlestown dating back to 1925, when James Sheehan, later nick-named Shiner, created a new sport for young men from nine to 20 years old. They would steal a nice car in Boston, come over the bridge, then race down Chelsea Street to Bunker Hill Street to Main Street. This **"loop"** around the one square mile of Charlestown was at speeds of up to 80 miles per hour; the drivers were chased by the Boston Police. Generally the word would spread throughout Charlestown – "there is going to be looping tonight." Pearl Harbor was the beginning of the end of the Loopers as most young men went off to war.

Top 25 Movies Set in Boston

1. The Departed
2. Good Will Hunting
3. Shutter Island
4. Spotlight
5. Mystic River
6. Now, Voyager
7. The Fighter
8. Manchester by the Sea
9. The Boondock Saints
10. The Social Network
11. The Verdict
12. Gone Baby Gone
13. The Town
14. The Friends of Eddie Coyle
15. Patriot's Day
16. The Equalizer
17. Pieces of a Woman
18. The Boston Strangler
19. The Out of Towners
20. The Thomas Crown Affair
21. Infinitely Polar Bear
22. Ted
23. Black Mass
24. Stronger
25. 21

List compiled by Stacker.com and ranked using IMBd user ratings.

Chinatown

Boston's Chinatown is a close-knit neighborhood and the only historic Chinese enclave in New England. Established in the late 19th century, it has evolved into a cultural and commercial hub for Asian communities, particularly Chinese and Vietnamese.

Part of the Chinatown neighborhood occupies a space reclaimed by filling in a tidal flat. The newly created area was first settled by Boston residents. Residential properties in this area soon became less desirable due to railway developments, so it was re-settled by a succession of immigrant groups, including Irish, Jewish, Italian, Lebanese and Chinese. Each group replaced the previous one, taking advantage of low-cost housing and job opportunities.

Chinese workers from California moved to Massachusetts in 1870 to break a strike at the Sampson Shoe Factory in North Adams, and in 1874 many of these workers moved to Boston. Many Chinese immigrants settled in what is now known as Ping On Alley. The first Chinese laundries opened on what is now Harrison Avenue, and the first Chinese restaurant, Hong Far Low, opened in 1875. During the late-nineteenth century, garment manufacturing plants moved into Chinatown, creating Boston's historic garment district, which was active until the 1990s.

Over the years, the neighborhood has faced challenges, including the impacts of the Chinese Exclusion Act of 1882, which limited immigration and resulted in a predominantly male population until the 1930s. The area underwent significant changes in the mid-20th century due to urban development projects, but it has remained a key center for Asian-American life in the region

31

Today, Boston's Chinatown is characterized by a dense concentration of Asian restaurants, markets, and cultural institutions. It is known for its diverse culinary offerings, which include Chinese, Vietnamese, Thai, and Japanese cuisines. The neighborhood features a variety of dining options, from traditional dim sum to modern Asian fusion restaurants.

Chinatown also hosts vibrant markets where visitors can find fresh produce, seafood, and traditional Asian delicacies, contributing to its role as a cultural and social hub for the Asian community in Boston.

The neighborhood is marked by the iconic paifang gate, a traditional Chinese archway that serves as the official entrance to Chinatown. This beautifully designed structure, gifted by the Taiwanese government in 1982, symbolizes the neighborhood's cultural heritage. Additionally, Chinatown Park, part of the Rose Kennedy Greenway, features unique landscaping, water fountains, and public art that reflect Chinese cultural themes.

Chinatown is one of Boston's most densely populated neighborhoods, where nearly 70 percent of the population identify as Asian, compared to about 9 percent citywide. The area has a median household income significantly lower than the Boston average, highlighting the socio-economic challenges faced by many residents. Overall, Boston's Chinatown remains a vital part of the city's cultural landscape, offering a rich tapestry of history, cuisine, and community life that continues to thrive in the modern era.

Do you Know Chinatown?

Boston's Chinatown is the third largest in the United States, behind New York City and San Francisco. It is the only remaining Chinatown in New England following the demise of Chinatowns in Providence, Rhode Island, and Portland, Maine.

Boston's Chinatown is known for its diverse **Asian cuisines**, including Chinese, Vietnamese, Thai, and Japanese. Popular restaurants include Pho Pasteur, Q Restaurant, and various dim sum establishments.

Chinatown has a **population density** of more than 28,000 people per square mile, making it one of the most densely populated residential areas in Boston.

The **Chinese Exclusion Act of 1882** significantly impacted the neighborhood's demographics, resulting in a predominantly male population until the 1930s.

The iconic Paifang Gate, a traditional Chinese archway, serves as the official entrance to Chinatown. Photo by Taylor Keeran on Unsplash.

Boston's Rainbow Swash

The iconic gas tank in Dorchester, covered in a bold rainbow swash, has greeted I-93 motorists since Boston Gas Company commissioned former nun and social justice advocate Corita Kent to create the design in 1971. The design, transferred to its present location in 1992 when the original LNG tank was torn down, now bears the National Grid name. The 140-foot tank had its share of controversy early on, criticized for supposedly featuring a profile of Vietnamese Leader Ho Chi Minh's face in its blue stripe as a protest of the Vietnam War, a claim Kent denied. The artist died in 1986 and is also known for the 1985 "Love" postage stamp.

Dorchester

Dorchester is the largest neighborhood in Boston, covering more than six square miles and home to a diverse population of more than 90,000 residents. Dorchester is bordered by South Boston to the north, Dorchester Bay to the east, and the Neponset River to the south. It comprises several smaller neighborhoods and commercial districts, including Uphams Corner, Fields Corner, and Codman Square. Dorchester Avenue runs through the neighborhood, connecting various business districts and residential areas.

Dorchester was originally founded in 1630 by Puritans from Dorchester, England, who arrived on the ship Mary and John. It was one of the first towns established in the Massachusetts Bay Colony and was a separate town until its annexation by Boston in 1870. The original settlement was located near what is now the intersection of Columbia Road and Massachusetts Avenue. The neighborhood has a rich history dating from the Colonial era. In 1633, Dorchester held the first town meeting in America, establishing a form of local government that would become common throughout New England. The Mather School, founded in 1639, was the first public elementary school in America supported by tax dollars. Important colonial-era buildings that still exist include the Blake House (c. 1648) and Pierce House (c. 1683). Dorchester residents participated in King Philip's War in 1675-76, a conflict between Native Americans and English colonists.

In 1804, the area known as Dorchester Neck (now South Boston) was annexed to Boston, separating it from Dorchester proper. The arrival

35

of the Old Colony Railroad in 1844 replaced stagecoach service and spurred growth in the area.

The arrival of railroads and streetcars in the mid-1800s led to rapid population growth, transforming Dorchester from a rural area to a streetcar suburb. The 1908 Chelsea fire propelled Jewish settlement in Roxbury and Dorchester, though this community largely moved out by 1970. By 1920, the population had grown to around 150,000. The area has seen significant changes over the years, transitioning from a rural community to a densely populated urban neighborhood, particularly during the late 19th and early 20th centuries due to industrial growth and immigration.

Much like Boston, Dorchester is home to unique neighborhoods, including Adams Village, Codman Square, Fields Corner, Lower Mills, Savin Hill, Jones Hill, Pope's Hill, Harbor Point and Neponset. Dorchester Avenue is the main artery of the neighborhood, lined with immigrant-owned businesses and commercial districts.

Today, Dorchester is known for its diversity, with a population that includes significant African American, Irish, Polish, Vietnamese, Caribbean, and Cape Verdean communities. Diverse dining options, including Irish pubs and Vietnamese restaurants, reflect its multicultural community. The neighborhood hosts various events and activities that reflect its cultural diversity and community spirit, with the Dorchester Day Parade, begun in 1905, attracting crowds every year. Numerous parks and cultural institutions attract locals and visitors alike.

Established in 1885, **Franklin Park** is a large 485-acre park that offers walking and running paths, tennis courts, baseball fields, a golf course and basketball courts. Home to Franklin Park Zoo, which has nine main exhibits with over 220 species of animals. Hosts the annual Kite and Bike festival, usually held the Saturday after Mother's Day.

The **John F. Kennedy Presidential Library and Museum** commemorates the legacy of President Kennedy. The **Edward M. Kennedy Institute** for the United States Senate is an educational center that explores the history and role of the Senate, providing interactive exhibits.

The **Dorchester Historical Society,** founded in 1843, is a volunteer organization that preserves the history of Dorchester and offers various programs and exhibits. It organized and celebrated the first **Dorchester Day** in 1904 to commemorate Dorchester's 1630 founding. The historical society maintains four properties that are open to the public to tour on the third Sunday of each month. **The James Blake House** (1661) on Columbia Road is the oldest home in Boston and one of only a few examples of Western England country framing in the U.S. The **William Clapp House**, home of the historical society, the **Lemuel Clapp House** and the **Clapp Family Barn** are located on 195-199 Boston Street.

First Parish Church of Dorchester, founded in 1630, is the oldest religious organization in present-day Boston. **All Saints Church**, designed by Ralph Adams Cram in 1892, became a model for American parish church architecture for the next 50 years.

Pope John Paul II Park Reservation is a 66-acre park with picnic facilities, soccer fields, and walking paths, offering beautiful views of the Neponset River. It was built on a former landfill and drive-in movie theater site. The park features a restored salt marsh and abundant wildlife, including snowy egrets and great blue herons.

The Strand Theatre is a historic venue that hosts various performances and events, contributing to the local arts scene.

The Walter Baker Chocolate Factory, established in 1765, was the first chocolate factory in the U.S. The factory, located in Lower Mills, was converted to housing in multiple phases starting in the 1980s. The conversion preserved many historic elements while modernizing the spaces and has been recognized for its preservation efforts.

The Boston Little Saigon Cultural District, part of the Fields Corner neighborhood, is known for its concentration of Vietnamese-American shops and restaurants, the nation's first Vietnamese American Community Center, and the Luc Hoa Buddhist Center and Temple.

William Monroe Trotter, a prominent civil rights activist, lived in Dorchester. His house on Sawyer Avenue is now a National Historic Landmark.

In 1983, President Ronald Reagan visited the **Eire Pub** in Dorchester on short notice, based on a recommendation from a Secret Service agent originally from the area.

The phrase **"Originally From Dorchester"** first appeared publicly in a 1985 essay in the *Dorchester Reporter*, where the originator of the phrase, Steve Cosmopulos, expressed his frustration with people who downplayed their Dorchester origins. He envisioned **OFD** as a way for people to proudly declare their Dorchester roots. OFD is still popular today, displayed proudly on bumper stickers and social media groups.

Dorchester Park is a beautifully maintained 30-acre expanse listed on the National Register of Historic Places. It was constructed as part of Boston's Emerald Necklace in 1891 and has large areas of woodland, paved walkways, a playground, a baseball field and tennis courts.

The **Lower Neponset River Trail** is a 2.4-mile path stretching from the Port Norfolk neighborhood through various parks and natural areas. It offers scenic views of Neponset marshes and is ideal for running, biking, and walking. The **Neponset River Greenway** is a 5-mile trail featuring diverse scenery, including a salt marsh in Pope John Paul II Park and Tenean Beach. Accessible from the MBTA Red Line.

The **Chez Vous Roller Skating Rink** has been a staple in the neighborhood for over 80 years, serving generations of families and roller skaters.

Dorchester boasts three neighborhood beaches. **Savin Hill Beach** includes a playground, sports fields, and a bathhouse. It's known for its scenic views and is suitable for swimming, although it is unguarded. **Tenean Beach**, the smallest beach in Boston, provides a tranquil setting along the Neponset River and scenic views of the Boston skyline. **Malibu Beach** allows swimming and has been restored to enhance its natural beauty. Facilities include a bathhouse and accessible features for visitors with disabilities.

Downtown

Downtown Boston has a rich history dating back to the city's founding in 1630. It was the center of colonial civic life and trade, with the Old State House serving as the seat of government. Many streets, such as Washington Street, trace their origins to the 17th century. The Great Fire of 1872 destroyed much of the area, leading to reconstruction in Victorian styles. By the late 19th century, early skyscrapers emerged in Downtown Crossing amid major department stores and financial institutions. The early 20th century saw a thriving theater district with ornate movie palaces.

Despite fires and urban renewal projects like the demolition of Scollay Square, Downtown Boston retains many historic landmarks like the Old South Meeting House, Faneuil Hall, and the Corner Bookstore. Its colonial roots, architectural heritage, and role as a commercial hub make it an integral part of Boston's identity.

Downtown Boston has been at the center of numerous pivotal historical events that shaped not only the city but the entire U.S. In 1630, the Puritans led by John Winthrop established the Massachusetts Bay Colony, with Boston as its capital. The settlement began around what is now Spring Lane, an alley way that connects Washington and Devonshire streets, where the first freshwater spring was discovered.

As the colony grew, several important institutions were established. In 1635, Boston Latin School, the oldest public school in America, was founded. The 18th century saw Boston become a hotbed of revolutionary activity. In 1765, protests against the Stamp Act took place near the Old State House. The Boston Massacre occurred on March 5, 1770, when

British soldiers fired into a crowd of protesters, killing five colonists. This event, which happened in front of the Old State House, significantly heightened tensions between the colonists and the British.

One of the most famous events in Boston's history occurred on December 16, 1773, when protesters, some disguised as Native Americans, boarded ships in Boston Harbor and dumped 342 chests of tea into the water. This act of defiance against British taxation policies, dubbed the Boston Tea Party, is considered a key catalyst for the American Revolution. The Revolutionary War began in earnest with the Battles of Lexington and Concord on April 19, 1775. While these battles took place outside of downtown Boston, the city played a crucial role in the events leading up to them. Paul Revere's famous midnight ride to warn colonists of approaching British troops began in Boston's North End. During the Siege of Boston (1775-1776), the city was occupied by British forces. The Battle of Bunker Hill on June 17, 1775, was a significant engagement during this period. Although technically a British victory, the heavy losses they sustained boosted American morale. The siege ended on March 17, 1776, when British troops evacuated the city. After the war, Boston continued to be a center of political and cultural significance.

The Old State House, which had been the seat of colonial government, became the state house of the Commonwealth of Massachusetts until 1798.

In the 19th century, Boston's downtown area saw significant development. The Old Corner Bookstore, built in 1718, became a hub of literary activity in the 1830s-1860s as the home of the publishing firm Ticknor and Fields. They published works by renowned authors such as Thoreau, Hawthorne, Alcott, and Longfellow. The 19th century also saw Boston become a center of the abolitionist movement. Many meetings and speeches opposing slavery took place in downtown locations like Faneuil Hall and the African Meeting House on Beacon Hill. In 1872, downtown Boston was struck by the Great Boston Fire, which destroyed much of the commercial district. However, this devastation led to a rebuilding effort that modernized much of the area. The Custom House Tower, completed in 1915, was Boston's first skyscraper. Throughout the 20th century, downtown Boston continued to evolve. The city played a significant role in both World Wars, with many troops departing from Boston Harbor. The post-war period saw urban renewal projects that dramatically changed parts of downtown, including the controversial demolition of the West End neighborhood in the 1950s.

In more recent history, downtown Boston has been the site of numerous political demonstrations and celebrations. The area has hosted victory parades for Boston's sports teams and has been the focal point for movements ranging from civil rights to anti-war protests. Today, downtown Boston remains a vibrant mix of historical sites and modern development. The Freedom Trail, established in 1951, connects many of the city's key historical sites, allowing visitors to walk in the footsteps of revolutionaries and witness the layers of history that have shaped this remarkable city. From its humble beginnings as a Puritan settlement to its role in the birth of a nation and its continued importance as a center of culture and commerce, downtown Boston's rich history is evident in its streets, buildings, and the spirit of its people.

Do You Know Downtown?

The **Old State House** was the center of civic life and the scene of intense debates about colonial rights and independence. Within its walls, prominent figures like Samuel Adams, James Otis, John Hancock, and John Adams argued against British policies. Visit the Old State House Museum at 206 Washington Street, where Washington and State streets intersect.

Following the outbreak of the American Revolution, British forces occupied Boston. The **Siege of Boston** lasted from April 19, 1775, to March 17, 1776, when the British were forced to evacuate the city.

Wander around behind **The Bell in Hand** and **The Point**, and you'll literally trip over the **Boston Stone**, inscribed with the date 1737. If the date carved into its front tells a true tale, this relic of colonial Boston

41

predates America's independence. The known origins of the stone are shaky. A rumor persists that it was used as a surveying instrument to denote the "center" of Boston; but this may not be true.

The Sacred Cod is a five-foot wooden reminder of early America's success in the native fishing industry and has been displayed in the House chambers at the State House since 1784.

The **King's Chapel Burying Ground** on Tremont Street holds historical importance for Boston and early American history: It is Boston's oldest burial ground, established in 1630 when the city was first settled by Puritans. Many notable early colonial figures are buried there, including: John Winthrop, Massachusetts' first governor, Mary Chilton, believed to be the first woman to step off the Mayflower, the Reverend John Cotton, an influential Puritan religious leader, and William Dawes, Paul Revere's fellow rider warning of British troops in 1775.

The **Grasshopper Weathervane** on top of Faneuil Hall was created by coppersmith Shem Drowne in 1742 for the newly constructed Faneuil Hall. Inspired by the grasshopper weathervane that crowns London's Royal Exchange, the weathervane is large – four feet long and 80 pounds – and is crafted of copper covered with 23-carat gold leaf. Its glass eyes allow light to shine through and its belly is a time capsule, containing historical items including coins, old newspapers, and messages from various Boston mayors.

Boston Common is the oldest public park in the U.S., established in 1634. The Common has historically served various purposes, including a grazing area for cattle and a training ground for the military. Today, it provides an open green space for residents and visitors.

On June 2, 1875, Alexander Graham Bell and Thomas A. Watson transmitted sound over wires from a fifth floor garret on what was then 109 Court Street. The first successful sound transmission – the famous "Mr. Watson, come here, I want to see you" – happened the following year on March 10, 1876, and gave Boston the title **"Birthplace of The Telephone."**

On July 18, 1776, the **Declaration of Independence** was first read to the citizens of Boston from the balcony of the Old State House, marking a significant moment in the city's revolutionary history.

In 1852, the **Tremont Temple** burned down and had to be rebuilt. It happened again in 1879 and then again in 1893. The current version of the Tremont Temple was built in 1896 and stands in the same spot as the original. It's a massive, golden stone building –actively used as a church seating a couple of thousand people – and is on the Freedom Trail.

Crispus Atticus, a man of African and Native Amercian descent, was the first to fall in the Boston Massacre, an act of protest widely viewed as a turning point on the road to the American Revolution.

Originally made of wood, the **State House Dome** was covered in copper by Paul Revere's company in 1802 due to leaks. It was later painted yellow and gilded with gold leaf in 1874. During World War II, the dome was painted black to prevent reflections during blackouts to protect against potential bombings. It was re-gilded with 23k gold in 1997. The **main doors of the State House** are only opened on three specific occasions: when the President of the U.S. or a foreign head of state visits, when a governor leaves office on their last day (known as the "Long Walk" tradition), and when a regimental flag is returned from battle. This last occasion hasn't occurred since the Vietnam War, as flags are now returned to Washington, D.C.

Founded in 1807, the **Boston Athenaeum** is one of the country's oldest and most distinguished independent libraries, and perhaps one of the most beautiful buildings in Boston. With a circulating collection of more than half a million books dating from the early 1800s to present-day best sellers and 100,000 works of art, the library is a must-visit for readers and art lovers alike. The library requires a membership to visit, but Day Passes are available for $40 per person.

The tank at the **Boston Aquarium** is 40 feet wide and has a depth of 26 feet, holding 200,000 gallons of seawater. This makes it one of the largest aquarium tanks in the world, designed to simulate a Caribbean coral reef ecosystem.

Boston Murals

The City of Boston has worked with artists and community members to create new murals, and has created an online map to pinpoint their locations and inspire people to visit them in person. This is an ongoing project, and there are many more murals to be added. This is part of an initiative to promote public art in Boston. Some of the murals were completed by the Mayor's Mural Crew, a program started in 1991, providing summer jobs aimed at covering graffiti with murals painted and designed by high school students. **Murals pictured below adorn buildings on Blue Hill Ave., Dorchester, and Birch St., Roslindale.**

boston.gov/departments/arts-and-culture/boston-mural-map

East Boston

Nicknamed "Eastie," East Boson was annexed by the city of Boston in 1637. The landmass that is East Boston today originally comprised five islands east of the Malden, Mystic, and Charles Rivers, and across the harbor from Boston. These islands included: Noddle's; Hog's; Governor's; Bird; and Apple. The town of East Boston was first developed on Noddle's, the largest of the islands and a noted source of timber and grazing land, used for farming by English colonists throughout the 18th century.

As early as 1801, William Sumner proposed that the Federal government create a turnpike to connect Massachusetts's North Shore (along with Sumner's property on Noddle's) to Boston, saying such a road would create a valuable, direct route across Boston's harbor, making it easier for Boston, at the time an isolated peninsula surrounded by water, to expand. When this plan was rejected in favor of a route through Chelsea, Sumner moved onto other plans to improve Noddle's value.

By 1833, Sumner and partners Steven White and Francis J. Oliver had purchased half of Noddle's acreage. Together, they founded the East Boston Company and continued to consolidate additional landholdings until they had complete control over the island. Anticipating population growth, they adopted a grid street plan, the first planned neighborhood in the city. Jeffries Point, located at the southern end of the peninsula that faced Boston, was the earliest area of East Boston to be settled.

A bridge to Chelsea was built, roads were laid out, and houses were built. Much of this activity was spurred by the formation of the East Boston Lumber Company. During this period, the Boston Sugar Refinery,

45

East Boston's first manufacturing establishment – and the creator of white granulated sugar – was founded. In the mid-1830s, the company made several investments to further East Boston's development and continued attempts to get the Eastern Railroad to come to East Boston. The Maverick and East Boston ferries began service from Lewis Wharf on the mainland to East Boston. The ferry service from Noddle's Island was replaced in 1904 by the streetcar tunnel that became the MBTA Blue Line, the first underwater tunnel in North America.

East Boston long provided homes for immigrants, including Irish, Russian Jews and later, Italians. From 1920 to 1954, East Boston was the site of the East Boston Immigration Station, the regional immigration hub for Boston and the surrounding area. A once Italian dominated community, East Boston has demographically changed to reflect a diverse population of immigrants. After the 1990s, the neighborhood witnessed growing numbers of Latin American immigrants who now make up over 50 percent of the population.

The population of East Boston, a mere 1,000 residents in 1837, exploded to a high of just over 64,000, according to the 1925 census. The sudden rise is attributed to the immigrants who came from Southern Italy. Today, the neighborhood is home to more than 40,000 residents.

Do You Know East Boston?

During World War I, areas of East Boston served as an internment camp for Germans removed from ships. Period images show small, unfenced buildings and tiny gardens built by the internees, leading right up to the water's edge. Opposite the old Immigration Station were steps leading to East Boston, called the **Golden Stairs** because they represented the final climb to the golden opportunity in America for countless Europeans. The station operated from 1920 to 1954 as the region's immigration hub.

John F. Kennedy's great-grandfather was one of many Irish people to immigrate to East Boston. The **Kennedy family** lived on Meridian

Street before moving to a larger home on Monmouth Street. P. J. Kennedy purchased a home for his son, Joseph, and another for his two daughters at Jeffries Point.

The Madonna Shrine, which is the national headquarters of the **Don Orione** order, sits on top of the Heights. The statue, **Queen of the Universe**, is an exact replica of the one in Rome and was sculpted in 1954 by **Arrigo Minerbi**, in appreciation for the Catholic Church saving him and his family from the Nazis.

Suffolk Downs was built in 1935 in just 62 days with 3,000 workers, on the mud flats of East Boston. The track was the fourth in New England and an instant winner with racing fans.

Seabiscuit, the come-from-behind horse who lifted spirits and become one of the greatest thoroughbreds of all time, made his debut at Suffolk Downs five days after the track opened. He finished fourth in the first running of the Mayflower Stakes.

East Boston had more **Canadian-born** residents than any other section of Boston in the 19th century due to its ship building industry.

The **first subway tunnel** connecting East Boston to Downtown Boston opened on 1904 and was the first undersea tunnel of its kind.

The **Veronica Robles Cultural Center** located on Meridian Street in East Boston, is a vibrant hub for promoting Latino arts and culture. Founded by Veronica Robles, a Mariachi singer and cultural ambassador, the center fosters community action and economic growth.

East Boston is home to **Logan International Airport**, which was originally opened as Boston Airport in 1923. It was one of the first airports in the U.S. to have paved runways

In the 17th and 18th centuries East Boston was part of **Chelsea**. At that time it was known for farms and summer estates.

Maverick Square, a central and historic part of East Boston, is named after Samuel Maverick, one of the first European settlers in the area.

47

Wood Island Park, once a popular recreational area, was designed by the famous landscape architect Frederick Law Olmsted. The park was partially destroyed to expand Logan Airport.

In the 19th century, East Boston was a hub for shipbuilding, producing many famous clipper ships, including the **Flying Cloud**, which held the record for the fastest passage between New York and San Francisco for over 100 years.

Jefferies Point is a historic neighborhood offers stunning views of the Boston skyline. The neighborhood has a rich maritime history, including shipbuilding and port activities. **Piers Park**, located at 9 Marginal Street, opened in 1995 and offers beautiful waterfront views and recreational activities.

Santarpio's Pizza, a culinary landmark in East Boston, has been serving up legendary thin-crust pies since 1903. Originally established as a bakery, it began selling pizza in the 1930s and has since become an iconic destination for pizza lovers.

HarborArts is a non-profit art organization located on Marginal Street, and founded by artist Steve Israel in 2009. The organization uses public art installations to address the vital roles oceans play in the sustainability of the planet, and to promote creative and sustainable ways of living. Its main feature is an outdoor gallery hosted on the grounds of the Boston Harbor Shipyard, on Boston's Harbor Walk.

Belle Isle Marsh is the only remaining natural salt marsh within the City of Boston. A salt marsh is a low-lying, coastal area mostly comprised of native plants and grasses, which is flooded by ocean tides daily. The 359-acre Marsh is nestled between the urbanized East Boston District and Revere, and the neighboring town of Winthrop.

The **Boston Patriots** used the East Boston stadium next to the Logan Airport T stop as a practice facility in the 1960s.

The **East Boston Greenway** is a linear park built along an abandoned railroad right-of-way, linking several open space areas, including Piers Park, Memorial Stadium, Bremen Street Park, Wood Island Bay Marsh and Belle Isle Marsh. *Read more on page 133.*

1.   What is the name of this statue and where is it located?

2. Who does this memorial memorialize and where is it?

See photo answers on page 156

3. *Who lived in this house, with shamrock cutouts on its window shutters, on the Jamaica Way in Jamaica Plain?*

4. *What is this building and where is it?*

5. Who is depicted in this statue and where is it?

6. This plaque commemorates the location of the original Old Corner Bookstore. Where is it located?

7. *Who does this Memorial represent and where is it located?*

8. *Where is this site and what is its purpose?*

Fenway-Kenmore-Longwood

The Fenway and Longwood areas of Boston have a rich history spanning over 150 years, transforming from marshland to vibrant urban neighborhoods. The Fenway area was originally a tidal swamp and mud flat until the late 19th century. In the 1870s, the neighborhood started to take shape when land was annexed from neighboring Brookline as part of the Brookline-Boston annexation debate of 1873. The area's development was significantly influenced by landscape architect Frederick Law Olmsted. He designed the Emerald Necklace, a string of waterways and parks that helped shape the neighborhood's layout. This project involved filling in land and creating green spaces, which laid the foundation for the area's future growth.

By the early 20th century, the Fenway area had become a magnet for educational institutions. In 1907, there were twenty-two educationally focused organizations, including nine colleges and universities. Today, the area is home to numerous renowned institutions such as Northeastern University, Boston University, and the Colleges of the Fenway consortium.

One of the most iconic landmarks in the area, Fenway Park, was built in 1912. The first game at Fenway Park was played on April 20, 1912, the same week the Titanic sank. The park has since become a beloved symbol of Boston and a major draw for the neighborhood.

The Longwood Medical Area (LMA) developed into a world-class medical center over the 20th century. Today, it houses prestigious institutions like Harvard Medical School, Beth Israel Deaconess Medical

Center, and Boston Children's Hospital. The LMA now sees over 110,000 daily visitors for work or medical care.

The mid-20th century brought more development and character to the area. The Landmark Center was built and opened as a Sears, Roebuck and Company distribution center. The Green Monster, Fenway Park's iconic left field wall, was painted its signature green color.

In recent years, mixed-use developments such as Fenway Triangle and 1330 Boylston have added luxury apartments and retail spaces. The area has become a hub for biotech companies and medical research, capitalizing on its proximity to the LMA. As new and luxurious residential skyscrapers replace former fast-food restaurants and parking lots, the neighborhood's skyline and character change as well.

Nearby Kenmore Square, originally known as Sewall's Point, was originally a swampy area where the Charles River met the muddy marshes of Back Bay. The land was owned by Samuel Sewall, a Puritan judge who presided over the Salem witch trials in the 17th century. In the early 1700s, the area began to develop as a settlement, though it remained sparsely populated for the next century.

The transformation of Kenmore Square began in earnest in the mid-19th century. In 1852, a joint city-state-private project started filling in the 450-acre bay with gravel from Needham quarries. By 1890, the land reached Sewall's Point, which had been annexed to Boston from Brookline in 1874.

As the Back Bay developed into a well-to-do residential neighborhood, Kenmore Square became a commercial crossroads, with trolley lines and nearby railroads increasing use of the area. Elegant hotels, such as the Buckminster, Myles Standish, and Kenmore, opened to accommodate visitors.

The Kenmore area grew in popularity when Fenway Park was built in 1912, drawing large crowds to the area. The famous Citgo sign, a 60-by-60-foot beloved landmark, was erected in 1965. During the 1960s and 70s, Kenmore Square became a hub for rock 'n' roll, with clubs catering to the never ending supply of college students.

Do You Know Fenway-Kenmore-Longwood?

On the third Thursday of each month, the **Isabella Stewart Gardner Museum** opens its doors after hours for a night of merriment. Explore Gardner's enchanting home with a drink in hand (there's a cash bar), and try whimsical, hands-on activities inspired by current exhibits (a recent night included a calligraphy station). Whether there's music in the lush courtyard or discussions with artists and writers upstairs, the mood is magical; this is probably as close as you'll get to attending a cocktail party hosted by an early-20th-century luminary. Tickets are $5-$15; as a bonus, the thoughtfully sourced fare at the museum's Cafe G is surprisingly good.

Visit the Museum of Fine Arts and the Isabella Stewart Gardner Museum if you want to gaze upon million-dollar paintings for free. Every Wednesday night after 4pm, the Museum of Fine Arts allows guests to enter the premise for a strictly voluntary donation. And don't forget: everyone gets a free pass to the Isabella Stewart Gardner Museum on their birthdays (and Isabellas get in free forever).

Fenway Park, built in 1912, is MLB's oldest active ball park. The park has undergone numerous renovations and expansions over the years but its distinctive characteristics - such as the Green Monster and Pesky's Pole - remain. Fenway seats about 35,000 people, making it one of the smaller and cozier stadiums in MLB. Music fans also frequent Fenway Park, which began allowing concerts in 2003 when it hosted **Bruce Springsteen and the E Street Band**.

The **Longwood Medical Area** consists of Boston Children's Hospital, Dana-Farber Cancer Institute, Brigham and Women's Hospital, Beth Israel Deaconess Medical Center, the pharmaceutical company Merck, and the medical engineering oriented company Wyss Institute. This 213-acre district houses some of the most prestigious medical institutions in the world, offering exceptional healthcare, cutting-edge research, and advanced medical education. The LMA's impact extends beyond its borders, contributing significantly to Boston's economy and reputation as a global leader in healthcare and medical innovation.

The academic area, adjacent to the medical area, consists of **Harvard Medical School, Harvard Dental School** and **Harvard School of Public Health.** Emmanuel College, Simmons University, Wheelock College, Wentworth Institute of Technology and Mass College of Pharmacy make up a five-college consortium known as the **Colleges of the Fenway**. **Northeastern University** is just a few blocks away.

Boston Latin School, a public exam school for grades 7-12 and the oldest public school in the U.S., established in 1635, is steps away from Huntington Ave. on Avenue Louis Pasteur.

Fenway Health is a healthcare provider known for its comprehensive and culturally competent care, particularly for the LGBTQIA+ community and other underserved populations. Fenway Health is affiliated with Beth Israel Deaconess Medical Center.

Kenmore Square's **Lansdowne Street** is known for its nightlife, with various clubs, bars and proximity to Fenway Park making it a popular destination. The **Hotel Commonwealth**, a few blocks away, has symbolized the area's revitalization since its opening in 2002.

Boston University's main campus stretches along Commonwealth Avenue, with several buildings and facilities situated near Kenmore Square, including the BU Bookstore and Questrom School of Business. Nearby dorms and off-campus student housing contribute to the lively spirit around Kenmore Square.

Hyde Park

Hyde Park is the southernmost neighborhood of Boston located just under eight miles from downtown. Annexed to the city in 1912, its rich history dates back to the 1660s when it was primarily a farming area with a handful of small settlements and a population of about 50. The neighborhood developed into a paper and cotton manufacturing hub in the 18th century, and later became home to significant industrial operations, including the B. F. Sturtevant Company and the New York, New Haven & Hartford Railroad shops. After the Civil War and as a result of improved rail access, Hyde Park's population grew rapidly. In 1862, there were about 150 dwellings between Brush Hill Road and the Boston & Providence Railroad station. By 1865, this number had increased to 200 dwellings.

Hyde Park's involvement in the Civil War reflects its importance as a site of military preparation, political expression, and social tension during this period in American history. Hyde Park was home to Camp Meigs, an important Union Army training camp. The 54th Massachusetts Infantry Regiment, one of the first official African American units in the U.S. Army, trained at Camp Meigs.

The town of Hyde Park, named after Hyde Park in London, was officially formed in 1868 from parts of Dedham, Milton, and Dorchester due to a border dispute, and it was part of Norfolk County until annexed by Boston. In March 1870, a group of about 50 women led by Sarah Grimké and Angelina Grimké Weld took a bold stand for women's suffrage, marching to the Hyde Park Town Hall to cast ballots in the local election. As women were prohibited from voting at the time, this was a deliberate act of civil disobedience. The women were allowed to cast ballots, but their votes were placed in a separate box and not officially counted. But the symbolic act of voting, the first action of its kind in Massachusetts, brought widespread attention to the demand for women's suffrage 50 years before the 19th Amendment.

The section of Hyde Park bordered by Milton to the south and Dedham to the west is Readville, named after James Read, a resident and cotton mill owner. In the early 20th century, Readville hosted the Readville Trotting Park, a prominent harness racing venue, since repurposed into a multi-use warehouse property. Paul's Bridge, at the entrance to Readville near Milton, is one of the oldest bridges in the Commonwealth. Readville is home to several churches, including the historically significant Blue Hill Community Church, where prominent American Episcopal clergyman Phillips Brooks preached his last sermon.

Today's motto, "A Small Town in the City," reflects Hyde Park's suburban vibe, where you will still find warehouses intermingled with leafy streets. Hyde Park offers many recreational opportunities, including the George Wright Golf Course and numerous parks along the Neponset River. Public transportation, including the Fairmount and Providence Commuter Rail lines, provides access to downtown Boston. Home to about 35,000 residents and traditionally an Irish and Italian enclave, the neighborhood has seen an influx of various cultural groups, notably a large Haitian community that began settling in the area during the 1980s and 1990s. Its ongoing development and diverse population make Hyde Park an attractive place for residents seeking a balance between city amenities and a quieter lifestyle.

Do You Know Hyde Park?

The **Hyde Park Historical Society** is dedicated to preserving and showcasing the history of Hyde Park. Visitors can learn about the neighborhood's past through various exhibits and events.

Stony Brook Reservation offers outdoor activities such as hiking, picnicking, and nature walks. It features scenic trails, ponds, and picnic areas, making it a great spot for families and outdoor enthusiasts.

George Wright Golf Course, a public golf course designed by Donald Ross, provides a beautiful setting for golf enthusiasts. The course is known for its challenging layout and picturesque views.

It's hard to miss the influence of Readville native and former **Boston Mayor Thomas Menino** in the neighborhood, with everything from the YMCA to a wing of the Hyde Park branch of the Boston Public Library bearing his name. The **Thomas M. Menino YMCA** serves as a community hub, offering fitness classes, swimming, and recreational programs for all ages.

Most Precious Blood Church is an historic Roman Catholic church built in 1885 and known for its beautiful Gothic architecture. It serves as a spiritual center for the community and is a notable landmark in Hyde Park.

Logan Square is part of **Cleary Square**, the busy commercial district featuring a diverse mix of shops, restaurants, cafes and historic buildings. It is also home to essential community resources such as the Hyde Park Library and various local businesses, contributing to its role as a vibrant neighborhood center. Non-Profit **Hyde Park Main Streets**, made up of local businesses and volunteers, helps to create, maintain and promote this flourishing commercial district.

The movie *Glory* is a 1989 film about the 54th Massachusetts Infantry Regiment, one of the first African-American units in the Union Army during the American Civil War, which trained at Camp Meigs in Hyde Park. The film stars Matthew Broderick as Colonel Robert Gould Shaw, who led the regiment.

Fairmount Hill is characterized by its notable Victorian architecture, including Queen Anne and Georgian revival styles. The neighborhood was developed in the mid-19th century, initiated by a group known as the "Twenty Associates," who aimed to create a residential area in the then-rural landscape of Hyde Park. The first house was built in 1856.

Riverside Theatre Works, at 45 Fairmount Avenue, is a community theatre established over 40 years ago, now a vital cultural hub. Located in the historic French's Opera House, the venue offers a variety of performances, including youth productions, family-friendly shows, and plays aimed at adult audiences, and hosts community events. The theater boasts a 156-seat auditorium, a dance studio and rehearsal spaces.

The Everett Square Theatre also on Fairmount Avenue, has a rich history dating back to its opening in 1915. Designed by architect Harry M. Ramsay, the theater was built as a "moving picture house" and hosted vaudeville and live performances. Comedian Milton Berle performed there in 1925, leaving his signature backstage. The theater underwent several name changes over the years, including Fairmount Theatre and Nu Pixie Cinema. By the mid-1940s, it exclusively showed motion pictures. The theater closed in the mid-1980s and fell into disrepair, leading to various restoration efforts over the years. In 2008, organizations like Hyde Park Main Streets and Historic Boston Inc. began working on revitalization projects, including restoring the original signage and foyer. The theater's full restoration remains a work in progress.

The **Vertullo Building**, constructed in 1868, is likely the oldest surviving wooden commercial building in the Cleary and Logan Squares commercial area. The building is an excellent example of the Second Empire architectural style, popular in the 1860s, and reflects the period when Hyde Park was developing civic and commercial buildings along major transportation routes. Historic Boston Inc. (HBI) acquired the Vertullo Building in 2011 and completed a comprehensive rehabilitation in 2015.

My Grandma's Coffee Cake, Tutto Italiano and **Ron's Ice Cream and Bowling**, are just a few of the popular venues for food and recreation.

Jamaica Plain

Jamaica Plain, a neighborhood in the southwestern part of the city measuring 4.4 square miles and home to about 41,000 residents, was settled by Puritans seeking a rural residential community. The community seceded from Roxbury during the formation of West Roxbury in 1851 and became part of Boston when West Roxbury was annexed in 1874. Jamaica Plain became one of the first "streetcar suburbs" in the U.S. and is home to a large portion of Boston's Emerald Necklace, designed by Frederick Law Olmsted.

The name Jamaica Plain is derived from the indigenous American term "Mishawum," meaning "area surround by water." The district was initially populated by wealthy merchants and farmers who sought to escape the bustling and congested city center. They built large Victorian, Greek Revival and Federal style mansions and estates that still stand to this day.

Jamaica Plain played a significant role in the fight for American independence and the abolition of slavery. During the Revolutionary War, Jamaica Plain served as a refuge for those fleeing the British army. In the 19th century, the district was home to a large community of abolitionists and activists who fought tirelessly to end slavery and promote racial equality.

The wooded hills surrounding Jamaica Pond was the perfect setting for the country estates of Boston's wealthy families. Local farms helped provide Boston with fresh fruits and vegetables and the presence of a water supply gave birth to some small-scale industry. From 1795 to 1848, the Jamaica Plain Aqueduct Company supplied Boston with water from Jamaica Pond. Stony Brook, which at that time flowed above ground from Roxbury Crossing to Forest Hills, was another source of power and the development of the railroad along the same route fostered more growth. Even before 1850, the Stony Brook Valley was home to textile mills, printing shops, foundries, stone yard and lumber yards, and breweries.

In the late 19th and early 20th century, Jamaica Plain continued to grow and prosper, serving as a hub for transportation and commerce. The introduction of the electric streetcar system in the 1890s made it easier for people to travel between Jamaica Plain and other parts of Boston, leading to a population boom. During this time, Jamaica Plain became a diverse community, with a mix of ethnic and socio-economic backgrounds. By the turn of the 21st century, the neighborhood had attracted a large community of college-educated professionals, political activists and artists.

Today, Jamaica Plain is a vibrant, multicultural community that offers a mix of urban and suburban living. It boasts a wide range of cultural attractions, including the Arnold Arboretum, Jamaica Pond and the Southwest Corridor Park.

Hyde, Jackson, and Egleston Squares have significant Spanish-speaking populations, mainly from the Dominican Republic, Puerto Rico and Cuba. In 2016, the neighborhood between Jackson Square and Hyde Square was officially designated the "Latin Quarter" and is the center of local festivals, churches, and activist groups. The newspaper *El Mundo* is based in Hyde Square.

The elimination of redlining and the stabilization of the real estate market in the late 1970s and the redevelopment of the Southwest Corridor set the stage for gentrification that began in the 1990s. A hot real estate market has driven dramatic increases in the value of older homes in the Parkside, Pondside and Sumner Hill neighborhoods and conversion of some larger residential properties and older commercial buildings into condominiums.

Do You Know Jamaica Plain?

The oldest community theater group in the United States is the **Footlight Club** on Eliot Street.

Jamaica Pond is a glacial kettle pond and the largest body of freshwater in the city, covering approximately 68 acres and reaching depths of more than 50 feet. The 1.5-mile walking path around the pond makes it a popular destination for walking, jogging, and cycling, as well as for fishing, rowing, and sailing. Visitors can rent rowboats, kayaks, and sailboats from the Boathouse, which operates seasonally. The pond is stocked annually with trout, attracting anglers and nature enthusiasts alike, who can also spot various bird species, including ducks and swans. Jamaica Pond hosts community events, such as the Lantern Parade in October, where hundreds of people, many in Halloween costumes, walk around the pond with lanterns, creating a magical atmosphere of flickering lights.

The trees, shrubs and vines grown at the **Arnold Arboretum** - the living collection - is celebrated as one of the most comprehensive and best documented natural history collections of its kind. Rich holdings include temperate woody plants from around the world, with a particularly strong representation of the floras of the eastern United States and eastern Asia. Visit different areas of interest in the landscape, from microclimate hills to brooks to scenic overlooks of the Boston skyline. This 281-acre jewel in Olmsted's Emerald Necklace of parklands is both a research center and museum of Harvard University and a beloved public landscape open free to the public every day.

The **Forest Hills** section of JP is primarily residential, characterized by hilly terrain and wooded areas. **Forest Hills Station** is the southern end of the MBTA's Orange Line and is a stop on the Commuter Rail's Needham. A large portion of Forest Hills is occupied by **Forest Hills Cemetery**, an active burial ground that is also enjoyed as a 275-acre park and arboretum, recognized as one of the finest 19th-century rural cemeteries in the country. **Eugene O'Neill, E.E. Cummings and William**

Lloyd Garrison are among the famous people buried at the cemetery, which is listed on the National Register of Historic Places.

The **Haffenreffer Brewery** was established in 1870 by **Rudolph Frederick Haffenreffer**, a German immigrant who arrived in Boston after the Civil War. Rumor has it that the brewery once had a famous tap that poured out free beer day and night, filling the air with the aroma of hops. The top of the smokestack from the original brewery crumbled and was partially restored, leaving letters on its side reading "FENREFFER BREWERS." In 2016, a local artist installed a circular steel frame on the top with the letters "HAF," restoring the full name to the smokestack. The **Jamaica Plain Neighborhood Development Corporation** redeveloped the entire Haffenreffer complex, and one of its anchor tenants and investors is **The Boston Beer Company,** brewer of **Samuel Adams Beer**. The beer patriarch offers free daily tours of its brewery, where you can smell the hops and sample the results.

The giant cow head that adorns the old fire station on Centre Street beckons you inside the **JP Licks** flagship store. With its homemade ice cream and frozen yogurt known for its unique flavors, the shop has eight locations in Boston and nine in neighboring towns – all within 20 miles of its JP home base.

Sip through a session at the **Brendan Behan**, as cozy a pub as you'll find in Boston. It hosts a lively, long-running traditional Irish music session from 5 to 8 p.m. on Saturdays and offers a top-notch beer list. Bring in tasty Cuban sandwiches from **The Old Havana** across the street to pair with the pints, fiddling, and conversation.

Allandale Farm, on Allandale Road in Brookline, is a historic working farm straddling both Brookline and Jamaica Plain. Known for its commitment to sustainable agriculture, Allandale Farm connects the Boston area to its agricultural roots by growing a variety of plants and produce from seed to store. The farm spans approximately 105 acres and features a farmstand, greenhouses, and various agricultural operations. The farm offers an outdoor summer camp for children, community events and a Community Supported Agriculture (CSA) – a way to support the farm and get a share of the farm's harvest. In addition to produce, the farm offers gardening supplies, baked goods and upscale food products, and seasonal items like Christmas trees. The greenhouses, brimming with flowers and plants grown from seed, are fun to explore and open seasonally.

The **House at 17 Cranston** is an architecturally eclectic and distinctive 12-sided structure, with an unusual combination of Italianate and Gothic features. It was built around 1874 and is a distinctive landmark that overlooks Hyde Square from its high perch. The house was listed on the United States National Register of Historic Places in 1987.

Founded in 1868, **MSPCA-Angell** is the second oldest humane society in the United States. The center provides comprehensive veterinary services for more than 50,000 animals annually, a busy adoption shelter and a variety of animal behavior classes, including puppy training and socialization. Its campus previously housed Perkins School for the Blind, and then House of the Angel Guardian, an orphanage that operated there for several decades.

Jamaica Plain Open Studios is one of the most neighborhood and family friendly open studios around. Held over a weekend each fall, the event showcases a wide range of artistic disciplines, including painting, sculpture, photography, and mixed media. Visitors can engage directly with artists in their studio spaces, gaining insight into their creative process and inspirations.

Mattapan

Mattapan, a neighborhood located in the southern part of the city along the Neponset River, borders Dorchester, Hyde Park and Roslindale, and the town of Milton. It was originally inhabited by the Mattahunt Tribe and named Mattapan by the Neponsett Native American tribe. The name means "a good place to be" or "a good place to sit" due to its proximity to the Neponset River.

The Neponset River shaped the area's early history. Mattapan along with Dorchester's Lower Mills were the main fords of the Neponset River, allowing easy crossing from one side of the river to the other. Present day Adams St. and River St. connected Mattapan to fishing weirs at Lower Mills and the Neponset River outlet, while Squantum St. and Center St. in Milton connected it to shell fishing at Moswetuset Hummock and quarrying in the Blue Hills.

Mattapan began as part of Dorchester when settled by English colonists in 1630. Native Americans left a lasting impact on the layout of Mattapan, as many footpaths were adopted and transformed into roadways by settlers. In 1870, Mattapan was annexed by the city of Boston and began developing more rapidly in the early 20th century as streetcars and railroads improved access to downtown Boston. By 1960, Mattapan had a population of about 44,000 residents, 99 percent of whom were white and mostly Jewish. Demographic shifts occurred in the following decades as many white residents moved to the suburbs, resulting in a predominantly African American and Caribbean community today.

Today, Mattapan is a tight-knit community with residents living there for decades and with one of the highest rates of Black homeowner-ship in Boston. Its significant Haitian community is the largest in Massachusetts. According to U.S. Census data, the neighborhood has the highest rate (16 percent) of people who speak French, Haitian or Creole at home in Boston; nearly 12 percent speak Spanish.

The neighborhood features commercial areas primarily along Blue Hill Avenue and Mattapan Square, which host various businesses, including restaurants, retail shops, and health centers. Mattapan boasts several green spaces, including Franklin Park, designed by Frederick Law Olmsted in the 1890s and located in the geographical center of the city, connecting the neighborhoods of Roxbury, Dorchester, Jamaica Plain, Mattapan, and Roslindale. The 485-acre park remains Boston's largest open space and has miles of trails and playing fields, Scarboro Pond, the William Devine Golf Course, a renowned cross-country running course, the Franklin Park Zoo, White Stadium, the Elma Lewis Playstead and multiple playgrounds.

Today, Mattapan is recognized for its vibrant community life, diverse population, and ongoing public investment aimed at enhancing the quality of life for its residents. The neighborhood is home to a wealth of architectural gems, including Victorian-era houses, Colonial Revival-style buildings, and charming bungalows.

Do You Know Mattapan?

Forest Hills Cemetery is noted for its beautiful landscaping and serves as a significant cultural site in Boston. It was founded in 1848 and is listed on the National Register of Historic Places.

Mattapan Square is the heart of the neighborhood, with a bustling commercial hub offering a mix of restaurants and shops. Blue Hill Ave., the main thorough fare, is home to diverse businesses, from local bakeries and restaurants to clothing stores and specialty shops

Rise/Gateway to Boston welcomes people to Mattapan Square with two 19-foot tall statues by local artists. The late Fern Cunningham's sculpture celebrates the diverse history of Mattapan: A Native American figure holding a fish represents the Mattahunt tribe; a black Civil War soldier from Massachusetts' 54th Regiment; and Jewish, German, and Irish immigrants. A young family at the top of the statue represents Mattapan's current majority population of African-Americans and Caribbean immigrants. Across the way, Karen Eutemy's more abstract piece represents the future, illustrated through the symbol of a rising sun and mask-like faces below, belonging to no clearly defined racial or ethnic group.

The **Boston Nature Center and Wildlife Sanctuary** is a community nature center and wildlife sanctuary with two miles of trails, including a one-mile accessible trail, through meadows, woods, and wetlands. It is home to more than 150 species of birds, 40 species of butterflies, and more than 350 species of plants. The sanctuary also includes the **Clark-Cooper Community Garden,** which supports local families by providing fresh produce, is one of the largest community gardens in Boston with 300 individual garden plots. The sanctuary is located on the former **Boston State Mental Hospital,** which is also home to the **Olmsted Green** affordable housing initiative.

The Urban Farming Institute of Boston is a visionary urban agriculture organization committed to social justice and to bringing affordable, healthy food and healthy programming to the community.

The Edgewater Food Forest is a formerly vacant lot filled with lush fruit trees, berry bushes and mushrooms. Food forests mimic natural ecosystems, and focus on native food-bearing plants that provide habitat for insects and birds. This local forest is a collaborative effort between neighborhood groups, the city of Boston, and Boston Food Forest Coalition, a non-profit community land trust that has helped build 10 of these sites so far.

Harambee Park, designed by renowned landscape architect Frederick Law Olmsted, offers green space for recreation and community gatherings. It has been an integral part of the neighborhood since its establishment in 1898.

The Mattapan Branch of the Boston Public Library, recently renovated, serves as a community resource and offers various programs focused on education and sustainability.

The Mattapan Trolley, officially known as the Ashmont-Mattapan High-Speed Line, is a light rail line that operates between Ashmont Station, where it connects with the Red Line, and Mattapan Station, covering a distance of 2.6 miles. This line is notable for its vintage PCC streetcars, which were built in the 1940s and are the oldest operational vehicles in the MBTA system. It serves around 3,800 riders daily, down from pre-pandemic levels of about 6,600. Recent initiatives promise to modernize the Mattapan Line, which has faced criticism for its aging infrastructure and accessibility issues. The MBTA has committed $127 million to a transformation project.

Some of **Mattapan's churches have historical significance**, reflecting the neighborhood's changing demographics over time. For example, some former synagogues from when Mattapan had a large Jewish population have been repurposed as churches.

The Basilica and Shrine of Our Lady of Perpetual Help on Tremont Street in Mission Hill, also known as Mission Church.

Mission Hill

Just three-quarters of a square mile in size, Mission Hill is a vibrant neighborhood bordered by Roxbury, Jamaica Plain, Fenway-Kenmore, and Brookline. Known for its steep streets and stunning views of the city's skyline, the neighborhood is home to hospitals, including Brigham and Women's Hospital and New England Baptist Hospital, and is a popular area for young professionals and nearby college students. The neighborhood's main commercial areas, particularly Brigham Circle, bustle with shops, bars, and restaurants.

The area was first settled in the 17th century as part of Roxbury and became part of Boston in 1868 when Roxbury was annexed to the city. In the 18th century, the area consisted primarily of large country estates and apple orchards owned by wealthy Boston families. It was known as Parker Hill, named after the Parker family who owned large apple orchards on the hill.

Industry began to develop in Mission Hill as early as the 17th century, with the first brewery established at the foot of Parker Hill in the 1820s. By the 1870s, beer production, primarily run by German immigrants, had become the main industry in the area, with many breweries lining the Stony Brook.

The neighborhood's transformation accelerated in the mid-19th century. The introduction of streetcars in 1856 facilitated its growth as a residential area, allowing workers to commute to jobs in nearby industries. In 1870, the Redemptorist Fathers built a wooden mission church, then replaced it with a larger Roxbury pudding stone structure in 1876. Officially named Our Lady of Perpetual Help, the church was known by

71

most as "Mission Church," and became the namesake for the neighborhood. The church, located on Tremont Street, was elevated to basilica status in 1954 by Pope Pius XII and was designated as a Boston Landmark in 2004. It continues to serve descendants of Irish immigrant families who remain in the neighborhood, in addition to newly arrived immigrants from Ethiopia, Nigeria, and Haiti.

Mission Hill is notable for its architectural diversity, featuring a mix of historic homes, including brick row houses and triple-deckers. Most of the houses were built in a seven-year period around 1890, and many were constructed using abundant local puddingstone. The Mission Hill Triangle is recognized as an architectural conservation district, showcasing styles such as Second Empire, Neo Grec, and Queen Anne. This area has remained largely intact and is considered an important part of the neighborhood's heritage.

The first public housing development in Boston, Mission Main, was built in Mission Hill in 1940. The 1950s brought urban renewal efforts that displaced many residents and created dense tenements, leading to racial conflicts and crime in the late 20th century.

The establishment and growth of hospitals and universities near Mission Hill transformed it from a predominantly working-class neighborhood to a diverse community with a mix of students, medical professionals, and long-term residents. This change brought both economic development and challenges related to displacement and gentrification. Higher-income students and professionals moving into the area led to increased housing costs. This process priced out many long-time residents, altering the neighborhood's socioeconomic makeup. Many triple-decker homes were converted into condominiums and luxury condos and lofts were built.

Several universities established a presence in or near Mission Hill, impacting the neighborhood: Northeastern University, Wentworth Institute of Technology, and Massachusetts College of Art and Design are located in close proximity to Mission Hill. These institutions brought a large student population to the area, creating demand for off-campus housing and student-oriented businesses.

72

Today, Mission Hill has a population of 16,000 residents with a diverse demographic makeup: 42.7% white, 18.0% black, 17.5% Hispanic, and 14.1% Asian.

Do You Know Mission Hill?

Our Lady of Perpetual Help Basilica, referred to as "Mission Church," has been a central figure in the neighborhood since its establishment in 1870. The Roman Catholic church is renowned for its stunning architecture and serves as a significant community gathering place. Its Hutchings organ was installed in 1897 and was one of the first organs in the country to successfully use electric action, which Hutchings invented and patented. The organ has 62 stops, and close to 3,200 pipes. The spires, added in 1910, were designed by Swiss architect Franz Joseph Untersee, who also designed the rectory. It gained national attention when the funeral of Senator Edward M. Kennedy was held there in 2009.

The Mission Hill Triangle is an architectural conservation district that features a collection of 54 buildings constructed between 1872 and 1890. This area showcases various architectural styles, including Second Empire, Neo Grec, Queen Anne, and Renaissance Revival. The Triangle is recognized for its well-preserved historic homes, making it a notable landmark within the neighborhood.

The lower-east portion of Mission Hill had a **puddingstone quarry** that was actively mined throughout the 1800s. This sedimentary rock was used for constructing affordable housing, particularly for Irish and German immigrants who settled in the area.

Designed by architect Ralph Adams Cram and opened in 1929, the **Parker Hill Library** is a branch of the Boston Public Library. It has recently undergone restoration, enhancing its role as a community resource.

The Helvetia and Ester Buildings, located on Huntington Avenue, are residential apartment buildings that represent significant architectural styles in the neighborhood. The Helvetia is noted for its Queen Anne Revival style, while the Ester Building features Georgian Revival architecture.

While primarily a recreational space, the **Kevin W. Fitzgerald Park** is located on a hill top adjacent to the New England Baptist Hospital and offers stunning views of the Boston skyline. It is part of the area's urban landscape and contributes to the community's green space.

A much loved local spot for over half a century, **Mike's Donuts** is renowned for its delicious honey-dipped donuts deemed one of Boston's finest handmade pastries.

Orchard on Top of the Hill features more than 20 apple trees and provides beautiful views of Boston. It's perfect for a leisurely stroll or a picnic with friends and family.

Located next to the Mission Church, **Sheehy Park** offers a picturesque view of the Boston skyline, making it a great spot for relaxation and enjoying the outdoors.

The House of the Good Shepherd was founded in 1867 when five Sisters of the Good Shepherd were sent to Boston to establish a program for women in need. This initiative was part of the Sisters' mission to minister to women who required assistance and support. Located on Huntington Avenue, it served as a refuge for women and girls, providing care and support to various age groups. It served young children who could not be accommodated in overcrowded orphanages, pre-teen and adolescent girls, and adult women. In 1964, the decision was made to build a new home called Madonna Hall for Girls in Marlborough, Massachusetts. Today the land houses is an apartment complex, known as Mission Park.

The North End

The history of Boston's North End neighborhood is a captivating tale of transformation, immigration, and cultural heritage. As one of the city's oldest neighborhoods, the North End has evolved from a colonial settlement to a vibrant community that preserves its historic charm while embracing modern influences.

The North End's origins date back to the early 17th century when European settlers established the area as a bustling port and trading center. Its proximity to Boston Harbor made it a vital hub for maritime activities, shaping its identity as a hub of commerce and industry. Over time, the neighborhood's character shifted, with waves of different immigrant groups contributing to its cultural fabric.

During the 19th century, the North End witnessed a significant influx of Irish immigrants fleeing the Great Famine. This demographic shift blended Irish and Italian communities, each leaving an indelible mark on the neighborhood. Tenement housing became prevalent, with narrow streets lined by tightly packed buildings, fostering a sense of community amidst the challenges of urban living.

By the late 19th and early 20th centuries, the North End was a predominantly Italian enclave. In search of better opportunities, Italian immigrants infused the neighborhood with their traditions, language, and culinary practices. This period marked the beginning of the North End's association with Italian culture, a legacy that continues to define the neighborhood today.

One of the most iconic symbols of the North End is the Sacred Heart Church, built by Italian immigrants in 1888. The church served as a spiritual center and a focal point for the community's social and cultural gatherings. The feasts and festivals honoring various saints, such as Saint Anthony and Saint Lucy, became annual traditions attracting residents and visitors.

During the mid-20th century, the North End faced challenges due to urban renewal initiatives threatening its historic structures. While some buildings were lost, community activism helped preserve the district's character. Efforts to maintain the North End's identity led to its designation as a historic preservation district, ensuring the survival of its distinct architecture and cultural heritage.

In recent decades, the North End has undergone a process of gentrification while striving to balance its historical roots with modern development. The neighborhood's Italian influence remains strong, evidenced by the plethora of authentic Italian eateries, cafes, and bakeries that line its streets. Residents and tourists flock to the North End to savor traditional pasta, cannoli, and espresso.

The North End's significance as a cultural treasure is further underscored by landmarks like the Paul Revere House, the oldest surviving structure in downtown Boston, which provides insights into colonial life and the American Revolution. The neighborhood's waterfront location has also evolved, transitioning from a bustling port to a recreational area that attracts visitors for strolls and waterfront views.

The history of Boston's North End district is a captivating narrative of evolution and cultural fusion. From its origins as a colonial port to its role as a dynamic Italian-American community, the North End's story is one of resilience, preservation, and adaptation. Its historic charm, and modern vibrancy make it a cherished piece of Boston's tapestry, a living testament to the diverse waves of immigrants who have shaped the city's identity over centuries.

Do You Know the North End?

Nestled in the North End is an alley called **All Saints Way**. Behind an iron gate you can see the Wall of Saints, portraits ascending up the exterior brick wall of the adjoining building.

The **land area** of the North End is only 0.36 square miles.

Part of **Copp's Hill** was converted to a cemetery, called the North Burying Ground (now known as Copp's Hill Burying Ground). The earliest grave markers located in the cemetery date back to 1661. This historic cemetery, established in the 17th century, is the final resting place for many notable Bostonians, including Cotton Mather, a key figure in early American historical figure.

The North End became a fashionable place to live in the 18th century. Wealthy families shared the neighborhood with artisans, journeymen, and laborers. Two brick townhouses are still standing from this period: the **Pierce-Hichborn House** and the **Ebenezer Clough House** on Unity Street.

The Old North Church was constructed during the 18th century. Also known as **Christ Church**, It is the oldest surviving church building in Boston.

Three Italian immigrants founded the **Prince Macaroni Company**, in the early 20th century. Its building on Commercial Street, known as the Prince Macaroni building, was the first major conversion from commercial to residential use in the City of Boston.

In 1919, the Purity Distilling Company's 2.3 million gallon molasses storage tank burst open, causing the **Great Molasses Flood**. A 25-foot wave of molasses flowed down **Commercial Street** toward the waterfront, sweeping away everything in its path. The wave killed 21 people, injured 150, and caused damage equivalent to $100 million today.

In 1927, the **Sacco and Vanzetti** wake was held in undertaker **Joseph A. Langone, Jr.**'s Hanover Street funeral home. The funeral procession that conveyed Sacco and Vanzetti's bodies to the Forest Hills Cemetery began in the North End.

In 1976, the neighborhood welcomed **President Ford** and **Queen Elizabeth II**, who each visited the North End as part of the **U.S. Bicentennial Celebration**.

In 1934, the **Sumner Tunnel** was constructed to connect the North End to Italian East Boston, the location of the then-new Boston Airport (now Logan International Airport).

In the 1950s the **John F. Fitzgerald Expressway** (locally known as the Central Artery) was built to relieve Boston's traffic congestion. Hundreds of North End buildings were demolished below Cross Street, and the Artery walled off the North amount of commercial development. This activity was concentrated on Commercial, Fulton, and Lewis Streets. During this time the neighborhood also developed a red-light district, known as the Black Sea.

In 1859, tensions between the Catholic Irish immigrants and the existing Protestant community led to the **Eliot School Rebellion**. By 1880, the Protestant churches had left the neighborhood.

In 1849, a **cholera epidemic** swept through Boston, hitting the North End most harshly; most of the seven hundred victims were North Enders. The Boston Draft Riot of July 14, 1863 began on Prince Street in the North End.

Founded in 1879 as the North End Industrial Home, the school was officially incorporated in 1885 as the **North Bennet Street Industrial School**. Its initial mission was to help immigrants adjust to life in America by providing them with essential job skills and social services. The school's founder, Pauline Agassiz Shaw, was committed to a holistic approach to community service, offering a wide range of programs to support the immigrant population. Located on North Street, the school today offers intensive hands-on training in traditional trades and fine craftsmanship in these programs: Bookbinding; Cabinet and furniture making;

Carpentry; Jewelry making and repair; Locksmithing and security technology; Piano technology; Preservation carpentry; and Violin making and repair.

In the past, the North End was a stronghold for mafia activity, which has diminished throughout the years. From the 1960s to the mid-1980s, the **Angiulo** brothers were the dominant criminal group in Boston's North End. They were made men in the **Patriarca** crime family and controlled racketeering throughout Massachusetts. The neighborhood was known for mafia hit jobs as much as for its Italian cuisine. The mob's presence in the North End began in the 1910s and continued until 1983 when federal law enforcement arrested the Angiulo brothers.

The **Brink's Robbery**, a major heist that took place on January 17, 1950, at the Brink's Armored Car Company building on Prince Street, was meticulously planned by a gang of 11 for two years before executing it. The robbers stole approximately $2.7 million in cash, checks, and money orders (equivalent to over $30 million today). The entire robbery took only about 30 minutes to complete. The case was ultimately solved when one of the gang members, Joseph "Specs" O'Keefe, turned on his accomplices and confessed to the FBI in January 1956.

Paul Revere, age 15, was one of the original members of the Guild of Bell Ringers at the Old North Church.

Bova's Bakery on Salem Street is known for being Boston's only 24-hour bakery. For more than three generations, the Bova staff and family has produced award winning Italian pastries and treats from traditional Italian family recipes. Known for its genuine Italian baking styles and ingredients, the Bova family invites customers to the bakery to sample a taste of Italy.

Originally home to wealthy aristocrats, the North End transformed into a melting pot of cultures. After the Revolutionary War, Irish, Jewish, and Italian immigrants began to populate the area, with Italians becoming the predominant group by the early 20th century.

Ten Fun Boston Facts

1. It's the Birthplace of the American Revolution.
2. Boston Common is the Oldest Public Park in the country
3. It Has the Oldest Subway System in the U.S.
4. It Is Home to the First Public School
5. It Is Home to the First Public Library
6. It Has the Largest % of College Students in the U.S.
7. Boston Cream Pie Was Created at the Parker House
8. Boston Has 47 Miles of Shoreline & 34 Harbor Islands
9. The Zakim Bridge Is the Widest Cable-Stayed Bridge in the World
10. The BU Bridge Is the Only Place Where a Boat Can Sail Under a Train Going Under a Vehicle Driving Under an Airplane

Roslindale

Roslindale, located six miles from Boston's downtown area and bordering Jamaica Plain, Mattapan, Hyde Park and West Roxbury, is a vibrant residential community known for its close-knit neighborhoods, busy commercial square, world-renowned green space, and community-focused atmosphere. Just a 10-minute ride to Back Bay on the commuter rail, Roslindale's appeal lies in its high livability factor, spirited quirkiness and diversity. Roslindale has something for everyone.

Originally part of Roxbury, Roslindale seceded from Roxbury in 1851 and was annexed to Boston in 1873, evolving from a primarily agricultural area to the thriving residential community it became. Following its annexation to Boston, Roslindale began to develop as a "garden suburb." This concept allowed residents to escape the crowded and industrial areas of the city while maintaining easy access to urban amenities. The area's development was facilitated by improved train transportation, making it more accessible to city dwellers.

The area that became Roslindale was initially known as "South Street Crossing" or the "South Street District" of West Roxbury, because the Boston and Providence Railroad had a stop at South Street on its way between the two cities. However, John Pierce, a prominent local resident and Englishman by birth, thought the rolling hills, dales, and valleys of Roslindale reminded him of the bucolic town of Roslin in Scotland – and that name became the area's official moniker.

Transportation was the key ingredient to Roslindale's development. In fact, many Bostonians discovered Roslindale after coming to explore the site of a train wreck, and decided to stay. On March 14, 1887, a train

81

on the Boston and Providence Railroad was heading into Boston when it went over the Bussey Street Bridge, as it had done countless times before. The bridge collapsed, killing 24 and injuring more than 100 people. Later determined to be caused by design flaws, as opposed to a derailment, the accident became big news.

Roslindale's history is tied to waves of immigration, and the first significant wave of immigrants to the area were Irish fleeing the potato famine. They worked as field hands, domestics, and in various skilled and unskilled positions. By the 1870s, about a thousand Germans lived in Roslindale. They established cultural institutions like Germania Hall and the German Lutheran Church. Near the end of the 19th century, Italian immigrants began arriving in smaller numbers, often finding work in construction or clearing land.

Roslindale businesses and property values sank in the 1970s, largely due to school desegregation in Boston that led to "white flight" and the spread of shopping centers, which lured consumers from the local mom and pop stores. It was immigrants who helped revive Roslindale. In addition to Greeks and Syrian families, Lebanese, Haitian and Dominican professionals and workers began to arrive in the 1980s. In the mid-eighties, under the administration of Mayor Thomas Menino, the Roslindale Village Main Streets program ushered in an era of community investment and neighborhood engagement. The rebranding of Roslindale Square to Roslindale Village marked its current day transformation.

Today, Roslindale is celebrated for its cultural diversity, which is reflected in its local businesses and community events. The area hosts various festivals and markets, including "Salsa Dancing in the Square," fostering a lively community spirit. Roslindale Village serves as the local shopping district, centered around Adams Park, and is home to a variety of shops, restaurants, and a popular farmers market. Roslindale's population stays pretty steady at about 31,000 residents. Housing stock includes a mix of single-family homes, two-families, triple-deckers and small apartment buildings. It boasts a diverse population, with a significant number of families, young professionals, and retirees.

Do You Know Roslindale?

Adams Park is a small communal square in busy Roslindale Village, near the intersection of Washington Street and Cummins Highway. Its fenced-in green space is a welcoming area that hosts the **Roslindale Farmer's Market**, a seasonal market that features local produce and goods, providing a great opportunity to engage with the community and support local vendors. A memorial to honor local service members who died is nestled in one side of the park.

Roslindale Open Studios is a family friendly annual event held each October, showcasing local artists and taking place in artists' homes, studios, group sites and businesses. Hundreds of people turn out each year to explore the creative works.

The **Arnold Arboretum** is a 281-acre preserve that encompasses land in both Roslindale and Jamaica Plain. It's the oldest public arboretum in North America and is a National Historic Landmark. It offers trails and natural landscapes that have been enjoyed by residents for over a century. The Roslindale area of the Arboretum includes **Peters Hill**, which is the highest point in the Emerald Necklace park system, offering panoramic views of Boston. It's a favorite spot for viewing 4th of July fireworks, and for winter sledding. The **Weld Hill Research Building**, also in Roslindale, is a modern facility built to minimize the building's impact on the environment and its surrounding neighborhood. The facility supports the arboretum's scientific research and includes 12 greenhouses, state-of-the-art laboratories, growth chambers, study areas and offices.

The **Roslindale Substation**, built on Washington Street in 1911 by the Boston Elevated Railway (BERy), a predecessor to today's MBTA, was used for electrical conversion for streetcars until 1971. Designed by Robert S. Peabody of Peabody and Stearns in the Classical Revival style, the building sat vacant and boarded up for nearly 50 years. Recently renovated and repurposed for modern use, the Roslindale Substation's transformation into a vibrant community space exemplifies adaptive reuse of historic structures through community effort and innovative partnerships.

Sacred Heart Church is a Roman Catholic Church serving the communities of Roslindale and Mattapan. The church was established in 1893 by Father John Cummins, for whom Cummins Highway was named. It is designed in the Medieval Gothic style, inspired by European Gothic cathedrals and a common design for Catholic churches built in the late 19th and early 20th centuries. **Russian Orthodox Church of the Holy Epiphany**, located on South Street, is noted for its unique architecture and cultural significance within the community. It serves as a place of worship and community gathering for the local Russian Orthodox population.

In May 2018, **CSz Boston** and **Riot Improv** collaborated to open **The Rozzie Square Theater**, making Roslindale the official home for ComedySportz in New England and the new home for Riot Improv, relocating from Jamaica Plain. The theater is the only brick-and-mortar comedy club in Boston owned by a Woman and Asian American. It's a popular venue for improv comedy, and is known for its engaging performances and classes. It receives high ratings for its talent and atmosphere.

Long before restaurants such as **Delfino, 753 South and Sophia's Grotto,** to name just a few, made Roslindale a dining destination, generations of families flocked to the **Pleasant Café** on Washington Street for pizza served all day, every day. Its vintage vibe is so authentic that the 2023 movie *The Holdovers*, starring Paul Giamatti, used the location to film its interior restaurant scenes.

The **Roslindale Branch Library** underwent an $11.7 million renovation that was completed in 2021. The 14,855 square foot renovation added 4,205 square feet of usable space to the branch. It was designed with feedback from the Roslindale community, modernizing the space and making it more accessible, while still paying homage to the building's unique blue coloring and circular interior.

Roxbury

Roxbury is a historically significant neighborhood and vital center of Black culture in Boston. It was one of the first towns founded in the Massachusetts Bay Colony in 1630, originally encompassing Jamaica Plain and West Roxbury. It was established by Puritan immigrants who came from England with Governor John Winthrop. Located three miles south of Boston, it was an important town for transportation and trade, as the only land route to the capital city led through it. In 1846, Roxbury was incorporated as a city, and in 1868 annexed by the City of Boston.

Characterized by its hilly terrain, Roxbury had valuable resources, such as arable land, timber, water, and Roxbury Puddingstone, which was quarried and used in many building foundations. During the 19th century, Roxbury underwent significant industrial development. The main industries during this period included breweries, with several operating in the area. Piano makers also set up factories in Roxbury, contributing to the neighborhood's industrial growth. Other important industries included iron foundries, rubber manufacturing, textile mills and cordage production. These industries transformed Roxbury from its earlier agricultural focus to a bustling industrial center.

The growth of these sectors was facilitated by improvements in transportation, such as the completion of a horse-drawn bus line in 1820 and the Boston-to-Providence Railroad in 1835. This industrial development attracted waves of immigrants and contributed to Roxbury's evolution into a diverse, working-class neighborhood, home to diverse immigrant populations, including Jewish and Irish communities.

During the early 20th century, Dudley Square, renamed Nubian Square in 2019, became a vital retail center with movie theaters, a bowling alley, and department stores. Ferdinand's, the largest furniture store in New England, was located here. In the 1940s and 1950s, African Americans began migrating from the American South to Roxbury. This migration made Roxbury a center of Black culture in Boston.

The Freedom House in Roxbury holds significant historical and cultural importance as a civil rights hub. Established in 1949 by social workers Otto and Muriel Snowden, the Freedom House served as a critical meeting place for civil rights advocates and community leaders. It hosted prominent figures, such as Martin Luther King Jr., Malcolm X, and President John F. Kennedy for discussions on equality and racism in Boston. Decades before the 1974 federal court order on desegregation, the Freedom House initiated freedom schools and protests to counter segregation and racism in Boston public schools. It functioned as an important social, educational, and political organization for the neighborhoods of Roxbury, Mattapan, Dorchester, and Jamaica Plain and was at the center of key political movements in Boston, including urban renewal efforts in the 1960s. Despite its historical significance, the Freedom House building fell into disrepair and recent efforts to save it highlight the ongoing struggle to preserve such important landmarks.

Roxbury is home to the Dillaway-Thomas House (c1750), one of the oldest structures in Roxbury. The building served as the headquarters of the Continental Army in 1775 during the Siege of Boston. The house is now a museum with exhibits of Roxbury's past and present history and its landscaped grounds are part of Roxbury Heritage State Park, operated by the MA Department of Conservation and Recreation.

Today, Roxbury is tight-knit community, home to many longtime residents and multi-generational families. Newcomers are enticed by its proximity to downtown and its architectural mix of Victorian homes, historic brick row houses and triple deckers. Roxbury has undergone significant revitalization efforts in the last decade, with new businesses and cultural initiatives that reflect its dynamic character and ongoing importance within Boston's urban landscape.

Do You Know Roxbury?

Roxbury Puddingstone was named the state rock of Massachusetts in 1983. The rock, whose geologic name is Roxbury Conglomerate, is a sedimentary rock formed millions of years ago. Unlike most towns, which were named after places in England, Roxbury (called Rocksbury early on) was named for the rock that was so prevalent underneath the area's sprawling fields. Described as a "pebble and cobble conglomerate," Boston residents likened its appearance to the fruit in pudding traditionally served in England during the holidays – hence its nickname. The Roxbury Presbyterian Church is a well-known example of a local church built of puddingstone.

Eliot Burying Ground is the oldest cemetery in Roxbury, and one of the three oldest of Boston's historic burying grounds, with the first interment made in 1633. This burying ground was the site of the Roxbury Neck fortifications. During the Siege of Boston, American colonists built a redoubt in 1775 to defend the road to Dorchester and the entrance to the town of Roxbury.

First Church of Roxbury is the oldest wood frame church in Boston, with the current building dating to 1804. The church is historically and architecturally significant as an example of ecclesiastical architecture in the early nineteenth century and for its role in the development of the Roxbury community from a rural, agricultural town to a wealthy Boston suburb and now a densely populated, majority Black urban neighborhood.

Hibernian Hall on Dudley Street is a brick building built in 1913 for the Ancient Order of Hibernians, an Irish Catholic fraternal organization. It is one of only two dance halls from the period to survive. It remained a gathering place for local residents through the 1960s until a non-profit job training center took over operation of the building. **Madison Park Development Corporation** obtained the building, renovated and reopened it in 2005. The grand ballroom, which seats 250 people, serves the community as the **Roxbury Center for Arts at Hibernian Hall**, a venue for theater, concerts, dances and more.

The **Shirley-Eustis House** was built in Roxbury in 1747 by William Shirley, Royal Governor of the Province of Massachusetts. The home is a grand example of English Palladian design. Governor Shirley and his family lived very public lives as representatives of the British Empire and the family, their house and grounds were cared for by a staff of enslaved Africans, indentured servants and sometimes idle soldiers. Visit the organization's website (shirleyeustishouse.org) for tour information and to view its online exhibit: *Enslaved Lives in the Shirley Household.*

The **Malcolm X Residence** is the childhood home of civil rights leader Malcolm X, and is significant for its historical context. Malcolm X spent part of his childhood in the Roxbury neighborhood of Boston, moving to this home as a teenager in the 1940s.

Elma Ina Lewis (1921–2004) known as the Grande Dame of Roxbury, was a prominent American arts educator and activist, renowned for her contributions to the cultural landscape of Boston, particularly within the Black community. Born in Roxbury to Barbadian immigrant parents, Lewis had a strong sense of racial pride and commitment to promoting African culture through the arts.

Roxbury Community College, located on Columbus Avenue, consists of six buildings on a 16-acre campus. RCC offers 24 Associate Degree programs and 6 credit-granting certificate programs, providing students with an education that leads to transfer to a four-year college or immediate employment. The campus operates the **RCC Media Arts Center** and the **Reggie Lewis Track & Athletic Center**, which hosts more than 90 high schools, collegiate and national track meets each year.

Nubian Square, located at the intersection of Dudley and Washington streets. is the primary commercial center of Roxbury. In December 2019, the square was officially renamed from Dudley Square to Nubian Square after a community-led effort to honor the ancient Nubian civilization. It's part of the Roxbury Cultural District, dedicated to preserving and promoting Black culture in the area.

South Boston

Known as "Southie" by locals, South Boston is a vibrant and histor-ically rich neighborhood situated south and east of the Fort Point Chan-nel, bordering Dorchester Bay. South Boston was originally part of Dor-chester and known as Dorchester Neck, with its land used primarily for farmland and grazing in the 17th and 18th centuries. It was annexed by Boston in 1804, evolving from farmland to a predominantly Irish Cath-olic working-class community in the 20th century, and more recently, to a desirable location for young professionals and families.

Castle Island has been the site of a fortification since 1634, when the town of Boston decided to build defenses farther out in the harbor. By the end of the 17th century, the fort had been expanded to create a cross-fire with the fort on Governor's Island. In 1701, the fort was improved with brick walls and 20 cannon positions, becoming known as Castle William.

South Boston's history had strategic importance during the Ameri-can Revolutionary War: at Dorchester Heights, where George Washing-ton's forces compelled British troops to evacuate Boston in 1776; and on Castle Island, where British forces occupied Castle William setting fire to the fort as they left. A new fort, named Fort Independence, was built on the island beginning in 1801. Fort Independence helped protect Bos-ton during the War of 1812. The current structure of Fort Independence was built between 1833 and 1851 and is considered the eighth generation of forts on the site.

Castle Island was originally separate from the mainland, but land reclamation in the early 1900s connected it to South Boston by 1928.

During World War II, the U.S. Navy used the site as a ship degaussing station. In 1962, the U.S. government gave Castle Island and Fort Independence to the Commonwealth of Massachusetts. Today, Castle Island is a 22-acre state park operated by the Massachusetts Department of Conservation and Recreation. It's now a popular recreation site offering walking trails, beaches, and tours of Fort Independence.

Throughout the 19th and 20th centuries, the neighborhood became a hub for industries such as glassworks, chemical manufacturers, foundries, and machine shops. The industrial growth attracted immigrant workers and their families, with the Irish becoming the dominant immigrant group in South Boston from the 1820s onward. The Irish established numerous churches and social organizations, which played a crucial role in maintaining the neighborhood's cultural identity

Early Irish settlers were often skilled craftsmen and business owners, with many settling in the Lower End between A and F Streets. The Irish population surged during the potato famine in the 1840s and grew again after the Great Fire of 1872 in Boston's Fort Hill neighborhood.

While predominantly Irish, South Boston also attracted other immigrant groups, including Canadians from the Maritime Provinces, Germans, Polish immigrants around Andrew Square, Lithuanian immigrants in the Lower End, a small community of Russian Jews and a small Italian settlement.

The Archdiocese of Boston opened several Catholic churches to serve the growing Irish communities. Irish social and charitable organizations flourished, including eleven chapters of the Ancient Order of Hibernians. The St. Patrick's Day Parade, which evolved from an Evacuation Day celebration, began in 1901.

South Boston faced significant challenges in the latter half of the 20th century as it became the epicenter of the desegregation and busing crisis of the 1970s, gaining a reputation for racial tensions and resistance to integration.

Do You Know South Boston?

Walking around **Castle Island** offers a unique blend of history and scenic beauty. This 22-acre peninsula, connected to the mainland since 1928, is home to Fort Independence, a historic fortification built between 1834 and 1851. Visitors can stroll along the Harborwalk, which encircles the island, providing stunning views of Boston Harbor and the skyline. The loop around the fort allows for close-up views of its impressive granite structure, while grassy areas nearby are perfect for picnicking or flying kites. The beach offers a refreshing spot to relax or take a swim, making it a popular destination for families. As you walk, you might catch sight of planes taking off from Logan Airport, adding to the lively atmosphere. The area is also ideal for biking and scootering, with accessible paths for all visitors.

Sullivan's – or Sully's – is the landmark concession stand that has operated at Castle Island since 1951, when Dan Sullivan, Sr. opened the stand to offer quality food at reasonable prices. Four generations of the Sullivan family have continually operated this go-to destination where generations of Bostonians have enjoyed hot dogs, fries, seafood and more with a front row seat for watching people, boats and planes go by.

The Saint Patrick's Day Parade has historical roots, first organized by Irish immigrants on March 17, 1737 to honor their heritage and the Patron Saint of Ireland. It coincides with Evacuation Day, marking the withdrawal of British troops from Boston on March 17, 1776. This dual significance adds layers of meaning to the festivities, as the parade not only celebrates Irish culture but also honors military history. The event typically attracts up to a million spectators, who line the streets dressed in a sea of green.

Constructed in 1865, the **Harrison Loring House** is a two-and-a-half-story French Second Empire style brick mansion with a mansard roof, located at 789 East Broadway. Built in 1865 for Harrison Loring, owner of the City Point Iron Works, a major South Boston shipyard, Loring lived in this house until 1894. The house is listed on the National Register of Historic Places and is designated as a Boston Landmark.

Located on the historic South Boston Waterfront, the **Seaport** is one of the fasted growing neighborhoods in the city, especially among young professionals. In addition to the harbor front view, the area boasts museums, restaurants, shopping, fitness studios, a luxury movie theater, an outdoor concert pavilion, and a harborwalk.

The Boston Tea Party Ships & Museum provides fascinating insight into the most famous event that led to the American Revolution and changed the course of history. The experience includes guided tours, interactive exhibits, artifacts, interpreters, recreated 18th Century ships, and the multi-sensory documentary "Let It Begin Here." Abigail's Tea Room offers fresh baked goods, spirits, and the five teas thrown overboard at the Boston Tea Party. South Boston is also home to the **Boston Children's Museum** and the **Institute of Contemporary Art (ICA).**

Southie beaches form a three-mile stretch of parkland along Dorchester Bay, and include **Carson Beach, M Street Beach, Pleasure Bay** and **City Point/ Kelly's Landing Beach**. Every New Year's Day morning since 1902, hundreds of L **Street Brownies** run into the icy waters of Carson Beach for their **annual polar plunge**. Wearing everything from traditional bathing suits to elaborate costumes, including Spiderman and Santa suits, the L Street Brownies – named for the L Street Bathhouse – are the second oldest cold-water swimming club in the country.

Boston's only **triathlon** takes place in South Boston, where participants swim from Carson Beach, bike down Day Boulevard, then run a winding course through Moakley Park. The race is USA Triathlon sanctioned.

"Southie" has been popularized in various forms of media, including films and literature, often portraying the neighborhood's unique character and close-knit community ties.

The South End

The South End of Boston is a neighborhood with a rich and diverse history. Originally a tidal marsh, the area was transformed in the mid-19th century through an ambitious landfill project that began in 1849. This expansion was part of a larger initiative to create new residential districts in Boston, which also included the filling of Back Bay. Architect Charles Bulfinch played a crucial role in designing the South End, laying out streets and creating residential parks inspired by English town squares. The neighborhood was initially envisioned as an upscale area for the middle class, featuring uniform five-story bowfront structures built with brick, slate, limestone, and cast-iron elements. However, the South End's status as a wealthy enclave was short-lived. Economic downturns, such as the Panic of 1884, combined with the development of other neighborhoods like Back Bay and Roxbury, led to a decline in the area's fortunes.

By the late 19th century, the South End had transformed into a tenement district, attracting diverse immigrant communities. Throughout the 20th century, the South End became home to various ethnic groups, including Irish, Italian, Jewish, and African American residents. It developed a reputation as a "Jazz Mecca" in the first half of the 1900s. The neighborhood faced challenges in the mid-20th century, with many buildings falling into disrepair.

In the 1960s, urban renewal efforts began, leading to the demolition of some dilapidated structures and the construction of housing projects. This period also saw the start of gentrification, as many homes underwent renovation. Today, the South End is known for its Victorian architecture, being the largest intact Victorian row house district in the country. It covers more than 300 acres and features eleven residential parks. The neighborhood was listed on the National Register of Historic Places in 1973. The South End has evolved into a diverse and vibrant community, home to families, young professionals, artists, and a significant LGBTQ+ population.

The neighborhood is home to numerous art galleries, theaters, and performance spaces, making it a hub for creative expression. The SoWa Art + Design District, located in the heart of the South End, is a must-visit destination for art enthusiasts. Here, you can explore a diverse range of contemporary artwork, attend art exhibitions, and even purchase unique pieces directly from local artists.

The South End is also known for its array of restaurants, cafes, and eateries that cater to every palate. From trendy farm-to-table restaurants to cozy neighborhood bistros and ethnic eateries, there is no shortage of delicious options to satisfy any craving. The South End is also famous for its lively farmers' markets, where you can find an abundance of fresh produce, artisanal goods, and locally sourced ingredients.

Despite its urban setting, the South End also offers plenty of green spaces for relaxation and recreation. The neighborhood is home to several beautiful parks, including the iconic Southwest Corridor Park, which spans over four miles and provides a tranquil escape from the hustle and bustle of city life. Whether you're looking to take a leisurely stroll, have a picnic, or engage in outdoor activities, the South End has a park to suit your needs.

Do You Know the South End?

The Cathedral of the Holy Cross on Washington Street incorporates bricks from the ruins of an Ursuline convent that was burned down during anti-Catholic riots in Charlestown in 1834. These bricks were used in the arch over the front door as a symbolic statement of Catholic

94

resilience. The cathedral's construction was initially delayed by the outbreak of the American Civil War. Ground was finally broken in 1866, and the building was completed in 1875. The cathedral functions as a parish church for multiple congregations, including English and Spanish-speaking groups, as well as Ethiopian, Eritrean, and Egyptian Catholics practicing the Ge'ez Rite.

The removal of the **elevated train** structure on Washington Street allowed for better visibility of the cathedral's architecture. The "El" had previously obscured views of the cathedral and deprived much of Washington Street of sunlight.

On January 18, 1964, Cardinal Cushing celebrated **a Memorial Mass for President John F. Kennedy**, and Jacqueline Kennedy was in attendance. Erich Leinsdorf, the conductor of the Boston Symphony Orchestra, chose Mozart's Requiem because, like Kennedy's life and work, it was left unfinished due to a premature death

Boston College and **Boston College High** both opened their doors on St. James Street in the South End in 1863. Boston College moved to Chestnut Hill in 1913 and Boston College left St. James Street for Morrisey Boulevard in Dorchester in 1953.

The Franklin Square House was located at 11 East Newton Street in the South End. It was originally built as the elegant St. James Hotel in 1868. In 1902, Universalist pastor Reverend George Perin transformed the former hotel into a residence for working women, with the vision of "providing a home for working girls at moderate cost." By 1913, it was claimed to be "the largest hotel for young working women and girl students in the world" and could accommodate up to 850 residents by 1920. In the 1970s the building was converted into the Franklin Square Apartments, providing 147 units of affordable housing.

Throughout the Jim Crow era, most hotels, restaurants, and entertainment venues in Boston excluded Black patrons. Many Black jazz musicians instead found accommodations in the South End's abundant rooming houses and private homes. **Duke Ellington, Count Basie, Dizzy Gillespie, J. C. Higginbotham, Clark Terry, Wardell Gray,**

Russell Jacquet, Fat Man Robinson, Percy Heath, Milt Jackson, and many other jazz greats performed and stayed in the South End. Sammy Davis Jr. stayed in so many different places during his frequent stops in Boston during the 1930s and 1940s that neighborhood residents made a game of speculating as to where he would be spotted. Louis Armstrong, Count Basie, and Duke Ellington frequently dined and rehearsed at Mother's Lunch, a restaurant, venue, and boarding house located at 510 Columbus Ave and run by Wilhelmina "Mother" Garnes until in closed in 1956.

Martin Luther King, Jr. lived in a boarding house at 397 Massachusetts Ave. while studying theology at Boston University. King resided in Boston from 1951 to 1954 to pursue his doctorate at Boston University School of Theology. During this time, he met Coretta Scott, who was completing her degree in music education in Boston, and the two married in 1953. King returned to Boston on many occasions, most notably in April 1965 to lead a march from Carter Playground in Roxbury to Boston Common, speaking out against segregation in schools and high rates of unemployment.

In the wake of the Federal Housing Act of 1949, the city secured funding to plan the seizure and demolition of the **"New York Streets"**; by 1957, 321 buildings were razed, and more than 1,000 residents, many Jewish, Italian, and West Indian families were displaced by new industrial buildings.

The Harriet Tubman House, a fixture in Black Boston since 1908, has been at its most recent location since 1975. In 1904, six Black women, including Tubman's friend Julia O. Henson, rented the first Harriet Tubman House at 37 Holyoke Street in the South End to provide shelter to other Black women who recently moved from the South.

The Cyclorama Building on Washington Street, built in 1884, is now operated by the **Boston Center for the Arts**. The building was commissioned by Charles F. Willoughby's Boston Cyclorama Company to house the Cyclorama of the Battle of Gettysburg, a massive 400-by-50-foot circular painting depicting the famous Civil War battle. Visitors would enter through a crenelated archway, walk along a dark winding passage, and climb a staircase to an elevated viewing platform to observe the panoramic artwork.

The South End of Boston emerged as a **prominent gay neighborhood** in Massachusetts starting in the 1970s and, alongside Jamaica Plain, became one of Boston's main gay communities during the gay liberation movement of the 1970s. The value of real estate in the South End began to grow after members of the gay community bought homes in the South End and rehabbed them.

The **dilapidated South End building,** at the corner of Massachusetts Avenue and Washington Street, formerly the **Hotel Alexandra**, historically the **Walworth Building**, was built in the 1870s and once represented the lap of luxury in turn-of-the-century Boston. The 50-room residential hotel was purchased by the **Church of Scientology** in 2008, but since the Scientologists haven't been able to raise enough money to do anything with it, there is now a proposal to build 50 condominiums, which has received its first approval in the process.

The **Hi-Hat** was a prominent jazz club from the late 1940s to 1959, situated on the corner of Massachusetts Avenue and Columbus Avenue, where the Harriet Tubman House now stands. The Hi-Hat was considered the focal point for modern jazz and name-band Black music in Boston during the early 1950s. **Wally's Café**, one of the oldest family-owned jazz clubs in the country, features live music every night, showcasing talented local musicians and a cozy atmosphere for jazz and blues performances

South End Burying Ground was established in 1810 as Boston's first burial ground for poor and working-class people. Located on Washington Street between E. Concord and E. Newton Streets, it is estimated to contain around 10,000-11,000 graves, of which 90-99 percent of are unmarked. Burials ceased in 1866 and only 11-20 headstones remain visible today.

Famous Quotes About Boston

"Boston is an oasis in the desert, a place where the larger proportion of people are loving, rational and happy."

Julia Ward Howe

"I call Boston home because it's where I started coming into my own."

Sasha Banks

"Boston is actually the capital of the world. You didn't know that? We breed smart-ass, quippy, funny people."

John Krasinski

"The spring in Boston is like being in love: bad days slip in among the good ones, and the whole world is at a standstill, then the sun shines, the tears dry up, and we forget that yesterday was stormy."

Louise Closser Hale

"Boston has it all: incredible sports, great people and culture, an amazing food scene, the ocean and so much more."

Pedro Martinez

The West End

The history of Boston's West End district is a tale of urban transformation, displacement, and community resilience. Once a vibrant neighborhood with a rich cultural mix, the West End underwent radical changes in the mid-20th century that reshaped its landscape and community dynamics.

The West End was settled as a working-class neighborhood in the 17th century. Over time, it became a melting pot of various immigrant groups, including Irish, Jewish, Italian, and Eastern European residents. This diversity contributed to the area's rich cultural tapestry and vibrant street life.

By the early 20th century, the West End was a densely populated and lively neighborhood. Tenement buildings housed families from various backgrounds and its central location made it a hub for commerce, with markets, shops, and theaters dotting the streets.

The late 1950s brought drastic changes to the neighborhood in the name of urban renewal. This redevelopment plan aimed to replace the old, densely populated tenement buildings with modern housing complexes and commercial spaces. Between the late 1950s and early 1960s, the West End's historic buildings were razed, uprooting families from their homes. The urban renewal process had profound social and cultural consequences. Families and communities were fragmented as residents relocated to other neighborhoods. The sense of belonging and identity that had defined the West End for generations was abruptly disrupted.

The construction of the elevated highway system, including the Central Artery, further transformed the neighborhood's physical landscape. Once-vibrant streets were replaced with highways, isolating the West End from adjacent areas and erasing its former pedestrian-friendly character.

In the aftermath of the urban renewal project, many former West End residents maintained a deep connection to their lost community. The West End Museum, established in 2004, showcases artifacts and stories that capture the neighborhood's spirit. The museum's efforts to preserve the history of the West End have contributed to ongoing discussions about responsible urban planning development and the need to balance progress with preserving historical and cultural identity. Efforts have been made to revitalize and reconnect the neighborhood with the rest of the city, but the scars of displacement and loss remain. The lessons learned from the West End's history continue to inform urban planning decisions and the importance of preserving the unique identities of communities within the larger urban fabric.

Do You Know the West End?

The West End was once one of Boston's most diverse and densely populated neighborhoods. In the early 20th century, it was home to a mix of immigrant groups including Armenians, Greeks, Irish, Italians, Jews, Lithuanians, Poles, Russians, and others. At its peak, the population reached approximately 23,000 residents.

Leonard Nimoy, famous for playing Spock on Star Trek, grew up in the West End. The West End Museum features a video of Nimoy sharing his memories of the neighborhood. The neighborhood was home to **Martin Lomasney,** an influential Irish-American political boss known as "the Mahatma." He ran his political machine from the Hendricks Club in the heart of the West End, providing social services and charity to poor immigrants in exchange for votes and support.

West Roxbury

West Roxbury is a neighborhood located in the southwest corner of Boston, Massachusetts. It is bordered by Roslindale, Chestnut Hill, Brookline, Newton, Dedham, Needham, and Hyde Park. With its leafy streets, single family homes with expansive backyards, community spirit and civic pride, West Roxbury has long attracted young families and Boston civil servants, and is considered a truly multi-generational neighborhood.

The area now known as West Roxbury was originally inhabited by the Wampanoag Indian Tribe before European settlement. Originally part of Roxbury, West Roxbury was established in 1630 and became its own town in 1851, in an attempt to remain rural, before being annexed by Boston in 1874. The area was historically agricultural, with a significant transformation occurring in 1848 with the arrival of the Boston and Providence Railroad, which created stops in West Roxbury and spurred residential development.

West Roxbury has been home to several significant historical sites and events. Westerly Burying Ground was established in 1683 to permit the local burial of residents of Jamaica Plain and the western end of Roxbury. When West Roxbury was still part of Roxbury, the town's burial place, now Eliot Burying Ground near Nubian Square, was too long a distance to travel from West Roxbury. Westerly Burying Ground served as this community's burial place well into the 19th century.

Brook Farm played a significant role in West Roxbury's history as one of the most famous utopian communities in 19th century America. Brook Farm was founded in 1841 by George Ripley, a former Unitarian minister, as an experiment in Transcendentalist philosophy. The community aimed to create a more balanced society where intellectual and manual labor were equally valued, and where individuals could pursue their talents while contributing to the collective good.

The farm attracted many prominent intellectuals and literary figures of the time. Nathaniel Hawthorne briefly lived there and later wrote "The Blithedale Romance" based on his experiences. Ralph Waldo Emerson, Margaret Fuller, and Bronson Alcott were frequent visitors. Horace Greeley, the famous newspaper editor, was also associated with the community.

Brook Farm established a school that became its main source of income and was known for its excellence. This educational emphasis reflected the community's commitment to intellectual growth alongside manual labor. Despite its short lifespan (1841-1847), Brook Farm had a lasting impact on American intellectual and cultural history: It represented one of the most ambitious attempts to put Transcendentalist ideals into practice and influenced later social experiments and communal living arrangements.

West Roxbury continues to preserve its history through organizations such as the West Roxbury Historical Society, founded in 1931, which works to document and share the neighborhood's rich past. Today, West Roxbury has a population of approximately 31,000 residents. The neighborhood's appeal lies in its spacious homes, family-friendly environment and proximity to Downtown. Today, the many bars that once lined Centre Street have been replaced by a cultural mix of cuisines - including Mexican, Thai, Korean and Middle Eastern - upscale bakeries, restaurants, breakfast places and an independent coffee shop.

The neighborhood features several wooded areas and parks, including Millennium Park, Hynes Field and Billings Field, which provide ample green space for outdoor activities like hiking, picnicking, and sports.

Do You Know West Roxbury?

The **Irish Social Club of Boston**, founded in 1945, it moved its headquarters to West Roxbury in 1978, reflecting the neighborhood's strong Irish Catholic heritage.

The **Bellevue Hill Water Tower** is one of the area's most recognizable landmarks. At 330 feet above sea level, the massive light green tank sits high on a wooded hill and is part of the **Stony Brook Reservation**. The tower is said to be the highest structure in Boston, and is a visual dividing line between West Roxbury and Roslindale.

Two prominent Catholic churches flank either end of **Centre Street**, the neighborhood's busy commercial thoroughfare. **Holy Name Church** features a striking Romanesque Revival architectural style, designed by architect Edward T. P. Graham, and completed in 1939. The church's dome replicates that of the **Basilica di San Clemente in Rome**. The church houses a distinguished pipe organ built by the **Wicks Organ Company** in 1938, recognized for its tonal quality and historical value. **Saint Theresa of Avila Church** is considered a "gem of Gothic architecture." Its light-colored stone structure features a prominent bell tower. The inside of the church features a wooden framework ceiling, an unusual feature perhaps intended to "lower" the soaring nave.

Millennium Park, located off of the VFW Parkway, includes walking trails, sports fields, a canoe launch and picnic areas. It's a significant urban park covering 100 acres. It was established on the site of the former **Gardner Street Landfill**, with construction beginning in 1994 and the park officially opening on December 7, 2000. The park was developed using land excavated during **Boston's Big Dig** project and was inaugurated by then-Mayor Tom Menino.

Westerly Burial Ground, (on Centre Street, in between Mount Vernon and LaGrange streets) was established in 1683 and is open daily. Eight veterans of the American Revolution and fifteen veterans of the American Civil War are buried here. One-third of its existing grave-stones date from the 18th century; almost half date from the 19th century, and about 20 from the 20th-century. The oldest gravestone, from 1691, commemorates **James and Merriam Draper**, members of a prominent West Roxbury family. Skillfully-carved headstones provide an historic record of three centuries of West Roxbury.

Colonel Robert Gould Shaw was born on October 10, 1837, in Dartmouth to a wealthy and prominent abolitionist family. When he was five years old, the family moved to a large estate in West Roxbury adjacent to **Brook Farm.** He was educated at private schools in New York and Europe, and briefly attended **Harvard University** before dropping out. When the Civil War began in 1861, Shaw enlisted in the **7th New York Infantry Regiment** and later joined the **2nd Massachusetts Infantry** as a second lieutenant. In 1863, Colonel Robert Gould Shaw, the leader of the **54th Massachusetts Regiment** (the first all-black company of soldiers in the Civil War), was killed along with 255 of his troops after an attack on **Fort Wagner, South Carolina**.

The Roxbury Latin School, founded in 1645, is one of the oldest independent schools in the United States and has a long-standing tradition of academic excellence. **Catholic Memorial** is a private, all-boys college preparatory school established in 1957 and run by the Congregation of Christian Brothers, under the auspices of the Roman Catholic Archdiocese of Boston.

The Shamrock Shootout, held on Saint Patrick's Day/Evacuation Day, is an annual street hockey tournament. What began with 100 participants has grown into a 650+ player tournament that stretches nearly one third of a mile along Temple Street and includes music, food and other activities. **The Corrib Pub Classic 5K** has grown significantly since its inception 30 years ago. It now attracts thousands of participants and serves as a fundraiser for local youth organizations and charities.

Fontaine's Chicken (on the VFW Parkway/Route 1), now the site of the new **Mission on Fire** restaurant, was renowned for its **iconic neon sign** featuring a waving chicken named **Topsy**. This sign became a beloved local landmark from the 1950s until it was taken down in 2005.

Discovering More About Boston Neighborhoods

The Boston Research Center (BRC) is a digital community history and archives lab based at Northeastern University Library. Its mission is to illuminate Boston's rich neighborhood and community histories through innovative technologies and collaborative efforts. The BRC emphasizes the history of underrepresented communities, aiming to expand understanding of Boston's long history through the perspectives of its diverse residents, both past and present. The center leverages new technologies to help Boston residents share underrepresented stories from their community's past and gain deeper insights into how this history shapes the present.

The center builds on Northeastern University Archives and Special Collections' commitment to making archives as useful as possible to the neighborhoods and underrepresented groups they originate from. The BRC works on interlinking digital historical materials (such as maps, photos, and texts) with data (like census information and commercial records) and analytical narratives to highlight important themes. The center focuses on unlocking historical analog and paper data through scanning and reformatting, enabling more robust large-scale analysis and computation of previously inaccessible information.

Boston Myths

The Curse of the Bambino: This relates to the long-held belief that the Boston Red Sox team was cursed after trading Babe Ruth to the Yankees in 1918. For over 86 years, the Red Sox were unable to win a World Series, leading fans to believe that the curse was real.

Ghosts of the Boston Common: Legend has it that the ghost of a woman haunts the Boston Common. Some people believe that she appears at night, dressed in Victorian-era clothing and searching for her lost child.

Secret Tunnels of Boston: Rumors about a vast network of tunnels underneath the city have circulated for years, but no one has found them. Some believe the tunnels were used by smugglers during the colonial era, while others believe that they were used by secret societies for meetings and rituals.

Boston Tea Party: One prevalent myth is that the Boston Tea Party was a protest against high taxes on tea. In reality, the protest was against the Tea Act, which granted a corporate tax break to the British East India Company and did not impose new taxes on tea.

Boston Accent: While some Bostonians do have a distinct accent, not everyone talks like a character from "Good Will Hunting." Many people who live in Boston come from all over the country and the world and do not have accents.

9. What is the term Bostonians use to describe this style of building?

10. What is the name of this stadium, what is its capacity, and where is it located?

See photo answers on page 156

11. What is the name of this building and where is it located?

12. Faneuil Hall was built on the waterfront of Boston. How did it move to its current location?

13. *This is a prisoner-of-war camp known as Camp McKay. Where was it located and who were the prisoners?*

14. *This is the Boston College Campus in the 1930s. What has replaced the lower reservoir shown in this photo?*

15. What is the name of this Church and where is it?

16. What are the biggest secrets held in the John F. Kennedy Library?

110

Impactful Events in Boston's History

Paul Revere's famous midnight ride on April 18, 1775, was not a solo mission as depicted in Longfellow's poem. Revere, along with William Dawes and Samuel Prescott, rode to warn the Massachusetts militia of the approaching British forces. Revere arranged for the signal lanterns in the Old North Church, but the signal was meant for him, not from him. He did not shout "The British are coming!" as the colonists still considered themselves British. Revere was captured before reaching Concord, so his mission to warn the militia's arsenal there was unsuccessful. The poem romanticized the event to inspire patriotism during the Civil War era.

The Siege of Boston (April 1775 - March 1776) was the opening phase of the American Revolutionary War. American militia forces surrounded the British Army in Boston after the Battles of Lexington and Concord. George Washington took command of the Continental Army besieging the city. After fortifying Dorchester Heights overlooking Boston in March 1776, Washington's artillery forced the British to evacuate. The 11-month siege ended in an American victory as British troops withdrew by sea to Nova Scotia, ceding control of Boston to the Patriots.

The Cocoanut Grove fire was a deadly nightclub fire that occurred in Boston on November 28, 1942, killing 492 people. It remains one of the deadliest fires in U.S. history. The overcrowded club had flammable decorations and locked exit doors, trapping patrons inside as the fire rapidly spread. The tragedy exposed major fire code violations and lack of safety regulations, leading to sweeping reforms in fire laws and safety standards for public venues. New requirements included outward-swinging exit doors, illuminated exit signs, emergency lighting, sprinkler systems, and flame-retardant materials. A memorial will be built in Statler Park at 243 Stuart Street in Bay Village, one block from the former Cocoanut Grove site at 17 Piedmont Street.

The Boston Molasses Flood occurred on January 15, 1919, when a large molasses storage tank burst in the city's North End, unleashing a wave of over 2 million gallons of molasses that swept through the neighborhood at an estimated 35 mph. The disaster killed 21 people, injured over 150, and caused immense property damage. The molasses wave crushed buildings, derailed a train, and left a sticky mess that took weeks to clean up. The tragedy exposed the lack of safety regulations and led to reforms requiring engineering oversight and inspections for construction projects. It remains one of Boston's most bizarre and devastating disasters.

Urban Renewal efforts in Boston starting in the 1950s had a significant and often detrimental impact on many neighborhoods and communities. The West End neighborhood, a densely populated working-class area, was almost entirely demolished in the late 1950s to make way for luxury housing and commercial development. Over 7,700 residents, many of them low-income, were displaced from the tight-knit community. Residents of the West End were largely uninformed about the urban renewal plans until it was too late, breeding distrust in the city's redevelopment efforts. Other neighborhoods like the North End and Roxbury also faced threats of demolition and displacement of residents during this urban renewal period.

These projects prioritized upscale housing and commercial development over affordable housing options for displaced residents. This led to overcrowding in the few remaining low-income areas like Roxbury as displaced residents had limited options for relocation within their means. The demolition of neighborhoods broke up long-standing social networks, community spaces like churches and markets, and erased cultural identities tied to those areas. Studies showed residents who were displaced suffered psychological trauma akin to grieving over the loss of their homes and communities. Major highway projects like the elevated Central Artery sliced through the urban fabric, isolating neighborhoods like the North End and contributing to a car-centric development pattern. While urban renewal was intended to revitalize Boston, the top-down nature of the projects and lack of resident input led to widespread displacement, loss of affordable housing, and destruction of social and cultural networks in many neighborhoods.

Desegregation of the Boston Public Schools, between 1974 and 1988, involved court-mandated busing of students to achieve racial integration. The initiative was a response to the Massachusetts Racial Imbalance Act of 1965 and aimed to rectify longstanding segregation within the school system. In 1972, the NAACP filed a class-action lawsuit (Morgan v. Hennigan) against the Boston School Committee, alleging racial segregation in public schools. By 1974, U.S. District Court Judge W. Arthur Garrity Jr. ruled that Boston schools were unconstitutionally segregated and ordered a busing plan to integrate predominantly white and black neighborhoods, requiring students to be transported across the city to attend school.

The implementation of busing was met with fierce resistance from many white residents, particularly in working-class neighborhoods. Protests erupted, leading to significant violence and unrest and confrontations between demonstrators and police. School enrollment dropped dramatically as many white families moved to suburban areas to avoid busing, which coined the term "White Flight." The busing plan remained under federal control until 1988 when it was deemed successful in achieving desegregation goals.

The busing crisis had lasting effects on Boston's demographics and educational landscape and influenced local politics for decades, shaping discussions around education reform and civil rights. A book that examines race relations in Boston through the lens of busing and is still worth reading today is *Common Ground: A Turbulent Decade in the Lives of Three American Families* by J. Anthony Lukas, published in 1985.

The Big Dig, officially known as the Central Artery/Tunnel Project, was a massive infrastructure undertaking that transformed the city's transportation system. Initiated in the 1990s and completed in 2007, it was the largest, most complex, and most technically challenging highway project in American history. Its primary objectives were to: replace the elevated Central Artery (I-93) with an underground expressway; extend I-90 to Logan International Airport via a new tunnel; and build a new bridge over the Charles River. The project featured numerous engineering firsts, including North America's deepest underwater connection; the largest slurry-wall application in North America; the world's widest cable-stayed bridge; and the largest tunnel-ventilation system globally.

The Boston Marathon bombing on April 15, 2013, had a profound impact on the city of Boston. Three people were killed and nearly 300 injured when two bombs exploded near the finish line. The attack shook the city's sense of security, but also demonstrated Boston's resilience and strength. In the immediate aftermath, Boston's emergency response was swift and effective. First responders, medical personnel, and civilians worked together to treat the injured and transport them to hospitals. The city's preparation and coordination helped save lives. In the days that followed, Boston came together in solidarity and the phrase "Boston Strong" emerged as a rallying cry. The community united to support victims and their families. Annual events like One Boston Day were established to honor those affected and to promote acts of kindness.

Women of Significance

Michelle Wu – Mayor of Boston

Michelle Wu is the current mayor of Boston, assuming office in 2021. At 39 years old, she is the youngest modern mayor of the city and the first woman and person of color to be elected to the position. Wu is the daughter of Taiwanese immigrants and a Boston Public Schools mom, bringing a unique perspective to her role. Wu's political career began on the Boston City Council, where she served from 2014 to 2021. During her time on the council, she achieved several firsts, including being the first Asian American woman to serve and the first city councilor to give birth while in office. As mayor, Wu has set ambitious goals for Boston, focusing on making the city more equitable, green, and livable.

Some of her key initiatives include: increasing affordable housing requirements for new developments; investing $2 billion in school construction and renovations; implementing climate-friendly policies for buildings and development; expanding early childhood education services; and creating new offices for Food Justice, Black Male Advancement, LGBTQ+ Advancement, and Worker Empowerment. Wu's progressive agenda has faced challenges, including criticism from business leaders and opposition to certain policies. She, however, remains committed to her vision of making Boston "the best place in the country for families" and addressing long-standing issues in the city. Despite the pressures of her role, Wu continues to push for change, keeping a close eye on the time she has left in office to accomplish her goals.

Lucy Stone – Abolitionist and Suffragist

Lucy Stone, a prominent 19th-century suffragist and abolitionist, had a significant impact on Boston's social and political landscape. In 1870, she moved to Dorchester where she continued her tireless advocacy for women's rights. Stone co-founded the New England Woman Suffrage Association (NEWSA) and served as its president from 1877 until her death in 1893. In Boston, Stone established the influential *Woman's Journal* in 1870, which became a crucial platform for the suffrage movement. This weekly newspaper, which she edited until her death, helped shape public opinion and rally support for women's rights in the city and beyond. Stone's presence in Boston energized local women's rights activists and connected them to the national movement. Her work with NEWSA and the *Woman's Journal* made Boston a hub for suffragist activity, influencing local politics and inspiring generations of activists in the city.

Barbara Fish Lee – Philanthropist

Born July 3, 1945, Lee is an American philanthropist who founded the Barbara Lee Family Foundation in 1998. Raised in a middle-class Jewish family in West Orange, New Jersey, Lee developed an early interest in politics, inspired by her suffragist grandmother. Lee graduated from Simmons College in 1967 with a degree in Education and French Literature, later earning a master's in Social Work from Boston University. Her transition to philanthropy came after her marriage to and subsequent divorce from investor Thomas H. Lee, which left her with significant wealth. The Barbara Lee Family Foundation's primary focus is supporting gender equality in politics through non-partisan research for women candidates. The Foundation has helped elect over 200 women across 37 states and supported major campaigns, including Joe Biden's 2020 presidential run that led to Kamala Harris becoming the first woman vice president. Lee's philanthropic efforts extend beyond politics. She has been a significant donor to Boston's Institute of Contemporary Art and was listed among Boston's Most Powerful Thought Leaders in 2014. Lee has contributed $2 million to over 400 women candidates and separately contributed over $2 million to PACs supporting Hillary

Clinton's 2016 presidential campaign. In November 2023, Lee announced plans to wind down the foundation's work by the end of 2024, marking the conclusion of a significant chapter in her philanthropic career.

Melnea Cass – Civil Rights Leader

Melnea Cass, known as the "First Lady of Roxbury," was a pivotal figure in Boston's civil rights movement and community development throughout the 20th century. Born in 1896 in Richmond, Virginia, Cass moved to Boston with her family at the age of five as part of the Great Migration. Cass's activism began in 1920 when she helped organize African American women to register and vote for the first time. Her involvement in Boston's growth and development spanned decades and touched numerous aspects of city life:

Cass served as president of the Boston NAACP from 1962 to 1964, organizing demonstrations against school segregation. She was a charter member of Action for Boston Community Development (ABCD), assisting those displaced by urban renewal. Cass founded the Kindergarten Mothers to encourage early education and fought for educational equity. She also helped form the Boston chapter of the Brotherhood of Sleeping Car Porters and advocated for better employment options for African Americans. As president of the Women's Service Club for more than 15 years, Cass worked to ensure women's access to social security and other benefits.

From 1975 to 1976, Cass chaired the Massachusetts Advisory Committee for the Elderly. Cass's tireless efforts earned her numerous accolades, including honorary degrees from prestigious universities and the title of "Massachusetts Mother of the Year." Her legacy continues to inspire, with Melnea Cass Boulevard and the YWCA in Boston's Back Bay named in her honor. Cass's commitment to improving Boston through grassroots activism and community engagement significantly contributed to the city's growth and development.

E. Virginia Williams – Founder Boston Ballet

E. Virginia Williams was a pioneering figure in American ballet, best known as the founder of the Boston Ballet. Born on March 12, 1914, in Salem, Williams began her dance journey at the age of five to overcome shyness. She trained in various dance styles and briefly performed with the Boston Opera company before focusing on teaching. At just 16 years old, Williams started teaching ballet and eventually opened several studios across Massachusetts, including the Boston School of Ballet. In 1958, she founded the New England Civic Ballet, which later evolved into the Boston Ballet in 1963, becoming the first professional ballet company in New England.

Williams was a multifaceted leader, taking on roles from teaching and choreographing to sewing costumes and selling tickets. Her dedication and vision caught the attention of George Balanchine, who became an artistic advisor to the company and recommended it for a crucial Ford Foundation grant. Under Williams' guidance, the Boston Ballet grew into a respected institution. The company held its first season in 1965 with 20 dancers and introduced its first performance of The Nutcracker in the 1965-66 season. Williams' commitment to contemporary composers and choreographers set the tone for the company's innovative spirit. In 1982, Williams transferred directorship to Violette Verdy but continued to serve as an artistic advisor. Her legacy lives on through the Boston Ballet's ongoing success and initiatives such as the ChoreograpHER program, created to support female choreographers. Williams passed away on May 8, 1984, leaving an indelible mark on American ballet.

Lucy Wheelock – Educator

Lucy Wheelock (1857-1946) was a pioneering American educator who played a crucial role in the development of early childhood education and the kindergarten movement in the U.S. Born in Cambridge, Vermont, Wheelock initially planned to attend Wellesley College but changed course after visiting a kindergarten class. Inspired by this experience, she pursued kindergarten training under Elizabeth Peabody's guidance. In 1879, Wheelock began teaching kindergarten at Chauncy-

Hall School in Boston, where she remained for a decade. Her innovative teaching methods gained attention and attracted visitors interested in observing her techniques.

Wheelock's most significant contribution came in 1888 when she established a training class for kindergarten teachers in response to Boston's introduction of kindergartens in public schools. This class evolved into the Wheelock Kindergarten Training School, which later became Wheelock College. As an influential figure in early childhood education, Wheelock served as president of the International Kindergarten Union from 1895 to 1899. She also chaired the Committee of Nineteen, which studied and reported on kindergarten methodology. Wheelock was a prolific writer and lecturer, contributing articles to educational journals and translating works by German educators. She authored several books, including "Talks to Mothers" and edited "Pioneers of the Kindergarten in America." Throughout her career, Wheelock advocated for the importance of early childhood education and teacher training. Her work laid the foundation for modern early childhood education practices, and her legacy continues through Boston University's college of education, BU Wheelock.

Phillis Wheatley – Poet

Phillis Wheatley was a pioneering African American poet who made history in colonial America. Born in West Africa around 1753, she was enslaved and brought to Boston in 1761. Purchased by the Wheatley family, she displayed remarkable intelligence and was educated by them, quickly mastering reading and writing. At just 12 years old, Wheatley began publishing poems, gaining fame on both sides of the Atlantic. In 1773, she became the first African American and only the third American woman to publish a book of poetry, titled "Poems on Various Subjects, Religious and Moral." Despite her literary success, Wheatley faced significant challenges after gaining her freedom in 1774. She married John Peters in 1778 but struggled with poverty and ill health. Wheatley continued writing until her death in 1784, leaving behind a legacy that inspired generations of writers and challenged prevailing notions about race and intellectual capability.

Amy Beach – Composer

Amy Beach (1867-1944) was a pioneering American composer and pianist from Boston. She was the first successful female composer in the U.S. and the first American woman to compose and publish a symphony. Beach was a child prodigy who made her public debut as a pianist in 1883. In 1885, she married Dr. Henry Harris Aubrey Beach, who restricted her performances but encouraged her composition. Despite these limitations, Beach achieved remarkable success. Her major works include the Gaelic Symphony (1896), Piano Concerto (1900), and Mass in E-flat (1892). After her husband's death in 1910, Beach resumed performing and toured Europe to acclaim. Beach composed more than 300 published works, including chamber music, choral pieces, and songs. She spent summers composing at the MacDowell Colony and was based in New York City and Cape Cod. Beach is the only woman composer whose name is engraved on the Hatch Shell on the Esplanade.

Ann Whitney – Sculptor and Poet

Anne Whitney (1821-1915) was a prominent American sculptor and poet. She began her artistic career writing poetry, publishing a volume in 1859, before transitioning to sculpture in the 1850s. Whitney was known for her life-size statues and portrait busts, often addressing abolitionist and feminist themes. She created notable works such as "Lady Godiva," "Africa," and statues of Samuel Adams, Leif Erikson, and Charles Sumner, which can still be seen in Boston. Whitney was an advocate for women's rights, abolition, and equal educational opportunities. She lived independently, sharing her life with Abby Adeline Manning in what was called a "Boston marriage." Despite facing gender discrimination in her field, Whitney persevered and became a respected artist. She established a studio in Boston in 1876 and worked well into her later years, creating sculptures of prominent suffragists and abolitionists.

Josephine St. Pierre Ruffin –Activist

Josephine St. Pierre Ruffin was a prominent African American activist, journalist, and suffragist born in Boston on August 31, 1842. She came from a wealthy family, with a white English mother and a Black father from Martinique. Ruffin faced racial discrimination early in life, being removed from a private school due to her race. She married George Lewis Ruffin at 15, and they briefly moved to England before returning to support the Union during the Civil War. Ruffin was a trailblazer in many ways. She founded the Woman's Era Club and published the Woman's Era, the first national newspaper for African American women. She was active in the abolitionist movement, women's suffrage, and civil rights. Ruffin also helped establish the National Association of Colored Women in 1896 and later assisted in founding Boston's NAACP chapter. Her legacy as a civil rights leader, publisher, and advocate for Black women's rights continues to inspire.

Susan Paul – Abolitionist

Susan Paul (1809-1841) was an African American abolitionist, educator, and author from Boston. Born to Reverend Thomas Paul and Catherine Waterhouse Paul, she grew up in a family dedicated to social activism. Paul taught at Boston Primary School No. 6 and the Abiel Smith School, where she educated African American children and instilled in them a commitment to social justice. In 1832, Paul formed a Juvenile Choir that performed at anti-slavery meetings and concerts. She wrote "Memoir of James Jackson" in 1835, which is considered the first biography of an African American published in the U.S. Paul was an active member of the Boston Female Anti-Slavery Society and participated in the temperance movement. Throughout her life, Paul fought against slavery through education, music, and writing. She championed African American intellectual achievement and devoted herself to her students and community until her untimely death from tuberculosis at age 32.

Mary Dyer – Quaker Activist

Mary Dyer was a prominent Puritan-turned-Quaker activist in colonial America, born around 1611 in England. She and her husband William emigrated to Boston in 1635, joining the local Puritan church. Dyer became embroiled in the Antinomian Controversy, supporting Anne Hutchinson's religious views. This led to her family's exile to Rhode Island in 1638. In the 1650s, Dyer converted to Quakerism while in England. Upon returning to Boston, she faced severe persecution for her Quaker beliefs. Despite being repeatedly banished, Dyer continued to return to Boston to advocate for religious freedom. In 1660, Dyer was sentenced to death for defying anti-Quaker laws. Given the chance to recant, she refused, stating, "In obedience to the will of the Lord God I came, and in his will I abide faithful to the death." Dyer was executed by hanging on June 1, 1660, becoming one of the "Boston martyrs" and a symbol of religious freedom.

Margaret Marshall – Chief Justice

Margaret Marshall's impact on Boston has been profound and far-reaching. As the first female Chief Justice of the Massachusetts Supreme Judicial Court, she authored the landmark 2003 Goodridge decision that made Massachusetts the first state to legalize same-sex marriage. This ruling not only changed the legal landscape in Boston but also sparked a national movement for marriage equality. Marshall's decision resonated deeply with Bostonians, influencing countless wedding ceremonies and fostering a more inclusive community. Her leadership on the court and her commitment to constitutional principles of equality have shaped Boston's legal and social fabric. Beyond her judicial role, Marshall has been an active member of Boston's civic life, mentoring law students, speaking at events, and contributing to local institutions. Her ongoing advocacy for civic engagement and social justice continues to inspire Bostonians, encouraging them to participate actively in democracy and fight for equality.

Dr. Mary Ellen Avery – Physician

Dr. Mary Ellen Avery (1927-2011) was a pioneering American pediatrician who made groundbreaking contributions to neonatal medicine. Her most significant achievement was discovering the main cause of respiratory distress syndrome (RDS) in premature infants - the lack of lung surfactant. This discovery led to the development of surfactant replacement therapy, which has saved the lives of more than 830,000 premature babies. Avery was a trailblazer for women in medicine, becoming the first woman to chair the pediatrics department at McGill University and the first female physician-in-chief at Boston Children's Hospital. She received numerous honors, including the National Medal of Science in 1991. Beyond her research, Avery was an advocate for improving access to care for all premature infants. She was known for her focused determination, good sense of humor, and commitment to mentoring women in medicine. Her work continues to have a profound impact on neonatal care worldwide.

Famous Quotes About Boston

"When I'm in Boston, I always feel like I'm home.
I almost cry I feel so good."

Luis Tiant

"In Boston, they ask, 'How much does he know?'
In New York, 'How much is he worth?'"

Mark Twain

"Boston is just a village, sprawling far and wide,
more human than New York City."

Frederick Engels

"We are Boston. We are America. We respond.
We endure. We overcome."

President Joe Biden

"This jersey that we're wearing today
doesn't say Red Sox. It says Boston.
This is our f-cking city."

David Ortiz

A Must Visit

These attractions offer visitors a chance to explore Boston's lesser-known sides, from hidden architectural gems to unusual museums and historical sites. They provide unique perspectives on the city's rich cultural heritage, scientific achievements, and quirky charm.

Public Open Night at Coit Observatory: Every Wednesday night (cloud cover permitting), the Coit Observatory at Boston University offers free public viewings starting at either 8:30pm. (spring and summer) or 7:30pm. (fall and winter). The hour-long viewing with professional astronomers last about an hour.

The Innovation Trail: A self-guided tour showcasing Boston's history of innovation, covering 21 stops throughout downtown Boston and Cambridge.

Long Crouch Woods and Franklin Park Bear Dens: Remnants of a former zoo in Franklin Park, offering a glimpse into Boston's past.

All Saints Way: A narrow alley in the North End adorned with an impressive collection of saint statues and religious iconography.

The Bleacher Bar: A unique bar situated beneath the bleachers of Fenway Park, offering a direct view into the stadium.

The Museum of Bad Art: A small and privately-owned museum dedicated to "art too bad to be ignored," showcasing quirky and unconventional pieces.

These sites offer a glimpse into Boston's rich and varied history beyond the well-known Freedom Trail attractions:

The Old Corner Bookstore: Built in 1718, this building was once home to famous publishers and is now preserved as a historic site.

The Winthrop Building: Boston's first steel-frame office building, considered the city's original skyscraper.

Boston Irish Famine Memorial: A memorial dedicated in 1998 commemorating the Irish Famine and its impact on Boston's history.

Mary Baker Eddy Library: Explore the life, ideas, and achievements of Mary Baker Eddy, who discovered and founded Christian Science. Eddy was a pioneer whose work touched the fields of religion, health, and journalism.

These hidden gardens and parks offer peaceful retreats where you can enjoy nature, relax, and escape the urban environment for a while. Each has its own unique character and charm, providing different experiences depending on the season and your personal preferences.

James P. Kelleher Rose Garden: This hidden gem in the Back Bay Fens has more than 200 varieties of roses and is particularly beautiful in late spring and early summer when its 1,500 roses are in full bloom.

Ramler Park: This small, hidden park in the Fenway neighborhood is known for its beautiful flowers and peaceful atmosphere.

The Garden of Peace: A memorial garden near the State House that provides a quiet space for reflection.

The Fenway Victory Gardens: One of the last remaining World War II victory gardens in the country, offering a unique mix of community gardening plots.

The Norman B. Leventhal Park: A hidden oasis in the heart of the Financial District, featuring a garden trellis and a fountain.

The Southwest Corridor Park: While not entirely hidden, this linear park stretches through several neighborhoods and includes community gardens and green spaces.

While Boston doesn't have many truly "secret" parks, there are several lesser-known, family-friendly green spaces that offer great experiences away from the typical tourist spots. These parks offer a mix of playgrounds, natural beauty, and unique features that make them great for family outings. While they may not be completely "secret," they're often less crowded than more famous Boston parks like the Boston Common or Public Garden, providing a more relaxed environment for families to enjoy.

The Esplanade: This beautiful park along the Charles River offers plenty of space for families to enjoy. It features playgrounds, walking and biking paths, and stunning views of the Boston skyline.

Peters Park: Located in the South End, this park offers a great mix of amenities for families. It has a playground, dog park, tennis courts, basketball courts, and a baseball field.

The Riverway: This linear park provides a pleasant walking path along the Muddy River. It's a great place for a family stroll or bike ride, offering a peaceful escape from the city bustle.

Martin's Park: This unique playground near the Fort Point Channel offers stunning views of the Boston skyline. It features a playship, jungle gym, and a long metallic tube slide that kids will love.

Mayor Thomas M. Menino Park: Located in Charlestown and the city's first fully accessible playground, it is packed with play features like a four-seat seesaw, a sit-down merry-go-round, and musical chimes. Parents can enjoy unobstructed views of Boston Harbor while the kids play.

Charles Bank Playground & Spray Deck: Situated along the Charles River, this playground is perfect for families. In summer, it features a spray deck where kids can cool off.

Street Names That Sing

Roslindale has Composer Streets

*(Off of Washington Street, near intersection
of West Roxbury Parkway)*

Beethoven Street
Brahms Street
Haydn Street
Liszt Street
Mahler Street
Mendelssohn Street
Mozart Street
Schubert Street

West Roxbury has Bird Streets

(Also off of Washington Street)

Bobolink Street
Grouse Street
Heron Street
Partridge Street
Starling Street
Thrush Street
Toucan Road
Willet Street

Lesser Known Gems

When people think of Boston, usually they think about the Boston Common, The Boston Public Garden, Faneuil Hall and other very well-known places. But there are many other gems in the City that are worthy of a visit and that will further increase your enjoyment of the City of Boston.

Brook Farm – West Roxbury

Brook Farm was a significant utopian experiment in communal living that took place in West Roxbury from 1841 to 1847. Founded by former Unitarian minister George Ripley and his wife Sophia, the community was inspired by Transcendentalist ideals and aimed to create a harmonious society that balanced intellectual pursuits with manual labor. The 175-acre farm was established as a joint stock company, promising participants a share of profits in exchange for equal work. Brook Farm's primary goals were to combine the thinker and the worker, guarantee mental freedom, and foster a community of cultivated individuals living a simpler, more wholesome life away from competitive institutions. One of Brook Farm's most notable features was its progressive educational system. The community's school was renowned for its modern approach, emphasizing personal responsibility and passion for intellectual work rather than punitive discipline. The curriculum included an infant school, primary school, and a six-year college preparatory course. Brook Farm attracted numerous intellectuals and reformers of the time, including Charles Dana, Nathaniel Hawthorne, and frequent visitors such as Ralph Waldo Emerson, Margaret Fuller, and Bronson Alcott. This association with prominent literary figures and thinkers has secured Brook Farm's place in U.S. social and cultural history. Despite its lofty ideals, Brook

Farm faced financial difficulties and eventually adopted some of the so-cialist theories of Charles Fourier. The community's decline was has-tened by a fire that destroyed its central building in 1846, and it was dis-solved in 1847. Today, Brook Farm is recognized as a National Historic Landmark, serving as a testament to the 19th-century utopian movement and the Transcendentalist philosophy. Its legacy lives on through its in-fluence on American literature, social reform ideas, and as an early ex-periment in alternative living arrangements.

Today, Brook Farm, on Baker Street, is a state park maintained by the Massachusetts Department of Conservation and Recreation. It is open daily from sunrise to sunset.

The Boston Athenaeum – Downtown

It is one of the oldest independent libraries in the United States and features a vast collection of books and artwork in a beautiful historic building. The Athenaeum's history reflects its evolution from a small lit-erary society to a major cultural institution. Initially, it moved through several locations before settling into its current building, designed by Edward Clarke Cabot and opened in 1849. The building itself is a Na-tional Historic Landmark, recognized for its architectural significance and historical importance. Major renovations have taken place over the years, including expansions to enhance its facilities and collections. The Athenaeum has many comfortable and inviting places to spend the day. Wi-Fi, well-lit work tables, cozy nooks, and lovely views of the city. $40 day memberships are available at the front desk or online. All are wel-come.

Courtyard Tea Room – Back Bay

Enjoy an elegant afternoon tea in the **Courtyard Tea Room** in the historic McKim Building of the Boston Public library in Copley Square. There is a 90-minute seating with a prix fixe menu presented to you in-side of a book. The afternoon tea service is set at $68 per person, and you can reserve your spot online.

The Mapparium – Back Bay

The Mapparium, located in the Mary Baker Eddy Library, is a remarkable architectural and artistic creation completed in 1935. This three-story-tall globe is constructed from 608 stained glass panels, each representing 10-degree divisions of latitude and longitude and is designed to showcase the world as it was at that time, reflecting historical geopolitical boundaries. Visitors enter the Mapparium via a 30-foot-long glass bridge, allowing them to walk through the interior of the globe and experience a unique, immersive perspective of the Earth. The Mapparium is not just visually stunning; it also features exceptional acoustics, creating a "whispering gallery" effect where sounds can be heard clearly across the space. This unique auditory experience enhances the feeling of being at the center of the world, as visitors can hear whispers from opposite ends of the bridge. Originally conceived by architect Chester Lindsay Churchill, the Mapparium was inspired by the desire to

present a global perspective in contrast to sensationalist journalism. It has remained largely unchanged since its inception, serving as both a historical artifact and an educational exhibit, now part of the "How Do You See the World?" experience at the library. At the Christian Science building, 200 Massachusetts Avenue.

The Warren Anatomical Museum – Longwood Area

The Warren Anatomical Museum is one of the oldest and most significant medical museums in the United States. Founded in 1847 by Harvard professor John Collins Warren, it houses a collection of over 15,000 anatomical and pathological specimens. The museum is renowned for its historically important medical artifacts. Notable items include the skull of Phineas Gage, a man who famously survived a large iron rod passing through his brain, and the inhaler used during the first public demonstration of ether-assisted surgery in 1846. Originally serving as a teaching tool for Harvard Medical School students, the museum has evolved to become a valuable resource for researchers and medical historians. It is currently housed within Harvard Medical School's Countway Library of Medicine. As of 2024, the museum's public gallery is undergoing renovations and is expected to reopen soon. Despite this temporary closure, the collection remains accessible to researchers by appointment. The Warren Anatomical Museum stands as a testament to the history of American medicine, preserving and showcasing the evolution of medical knowledge and practices over nearly two centuries.

The Metropolitan Waterworks Museum - Brighton

The Museum is a private non-profit educational institution housed in the historic Chestnut Hill High Service Pumping Station. This site, built in 1887, was pivotal in supplying water to Boston and is a prime example of Richardsonian Romanesque architecture. The museum opened to the public in 2011 and aims to educate visitors about the history and engineering of one of the nation's first metropolitan water systems. The museum features the Great Engines Hall, which showcases three massive steam-powered pumping engines that once pumped millions of gallons of water daily. These engines, designed by notable engineers, stand over three stories tall and represent significant technological advancements of the 19th century. The museum hosts various educational programs focusing on engineering, architecture, public health, and social history, connecting historical narratives to contemporary water issues. The museum emphasizes climate awareness and sustainable water management practices, reflecting its commitment to addressing environmental challenges.

The East Boston Greenway - East Boston

The East Boston Greenway, also known as the Mary Ellen Welch Greenway, is a linear park that will span approximately 3.3 miles upon its completion, transforming a former Conrail rail line into a vibrant pathway. It connects various neighborhoods and open spaces in East Boston, including Piers Park, Memorial Stadium, Bremen Street Park, Wood Island Bay Marsh and Belle Isle Marsh. The project is a collaborative effort among local advocacy groups and city planners, aiming to create a continuous corridor that promotes community engagement, neighborhood connectivity and environmental awareness. The trail features separate paths for pedestrians and cyclists, allowing for safe and enjoyable use by a diverse range of visitors, from runners to families. The greenway is characterized by its lush landscaping, with trees, wildflowers, and well-maintained parks that provide a scenic backdrop for outdoor activities.

The Ether Dome at Massachusetts General Hospital

The Ether Dome is a historic surgical amphitheater located in the Bulfinch Building at Massachusetts General Hospital. Built in 1821, it served as the hospital's operating room until 1867. The dome-shaped space features tiered seating arranged in a semicircle, allowing medical students and observers to watch surgical procedures. On October 16, 1846, the Ether Dome became the site of a groundbreaking medical advancement. William T.G. Morton, a local dentist, publicly demonstrated the use of inhaled ether as a surgical anesthetic for the first time. This event, known as "Ether Day," revolutionized the field of surgery and pain management. Today, the Ether Dome is preserved as a national historic landmark and teaching amphitheater. It contains several notable artifacts, including an Egyptian mummy, early surgical tools, and a painting depicting the famous first ether surgery. The space has been carefully restored to maintain its original architecture while incorporating modern technology for educational purposes. Visitors can explore the Ether Dome to appreciate its unique architecture, historical significance, and the pivotal role it played in medical history. The amphitheater continues to serve as a venue for lectures and meetings.

Spring Lane - Downtown

Spring Lane is a historically significant alleyway in downtown Boston that runs between Washington Street and Devonshire Street. Spring Lane is named after the Great Spring, a vital freshwater source that attracted the Puritan settlers to the Shawmut Peninsula in 1630. The availability of clean, abundant water from this spring was a primary reason for establishing the settlement that would become Boston. The area around Spring Lane formed the core of the early Puritan settlement. Important early structures, including the first church, market, prison, burying ground, and the house of the first governor, were all built near this location. Nearby landmarks that still stand today include the Old State House and King's Chapel. The Lane is marked with historical markers.

The Hatch Memorial Shell – Esplanade Back Bay

The Hatch Memorial Shell, located on the Charles River Esplanade is an iconic outdoor concert venue renowned for its stunning Art Deco architecture and vibrant cultural history. Designed by architect Richard J. Shaw, the structure features a semi-circular wooden shell that stands 40 feet high and 100 feet wide, with a stone platform that extends its width to 160 feet. The shell was dedicated on July 2, 1940, and has become a beloved gathering place for music lovers and the community at large. The origins of the Hatch Shell date back to the late 1920s when Arthur Fiedler, then conductor of the Boston Pops Orchestra, envisioned a space for free public concerts. The first temporary shell was built in 1929, but it was not until the 1930s that funding became available for a permanent structure through the estate of Maria Hatch, who left a trust for a public memorial. After several iterations, the current shell was constructed following the destruction of a previous version by a hurricane in 1938.Today, the Hatch Memorial Shell hosts a variety of events, including the annual Boston Pops Fourth of July concert, which attracts thousands of attendees. Over the years, it has featured performances by numerous artists and remains a vital part of Boston's cultural landscape, symbolizing community spirit and artistic expression.

The Gibson House Museum – Back Bay

The Gibson House Museum is a historic house museum located in Boston's Back Bay neighborhood at 137 Beacon Street. Built in 1859-1860, it was one of the first homes constructed in the newly developed Back Bay area. The house served as a residence for three generations of the Gibson family from 1859 to 1954. It preserves an exceptionally well-maintained example of a Victorian-era rowhouse, offering visitors a glimpse into 19th and early 20th century domestic life in Boston.

Notable features of the Gibson House include original architectural elements, furnishings, wallpapers, and family artifacts. Preserved public and service areas are viewable on guided tours, including a unique three-story glass-windowed ventilation system, and ice and coal sheds in the rear courtyard

The museum gained recognition as a Boston Landmark in 1992 and was designated a National Historic Landmark in 2001. Its significance stems from being the only Back Bay residence that retains its original architectural features and interior decorative schemes.

Visitors can experience the house through guided tours offered Thursday through Sunday. The museum also hosts special events and programming, including lectures and an annual Repeal Day Celebration. The Gibson House has been featured in several films, including *The Bostonians* (1984) and *Little Women* (2018), further cementing its place in Boston's cultural landscape.

Alley's End - Bay Village

Bay Village is Boston's smallest officially recognized neighborhood, characterized by its charming brick rowhouses and a tranquil atmosphere. Nestled between the South End, Back Bay, and Chinatown, it features a unique blend of residential and urban life. The neighborhood was developed in the 1820s by filling in mud flats, and its architecture reflects the craftsmanship of artisans who built homes in nearby Beacon Hill. Bay Village boasts narrow, tree-lined streets, many of which are paved with brick and illuminated by historic gas streetlamps. The area is known for its active community, which organizes events like clean-up days and an annual block party.

Alley's End is a charming hidden alley with a European feel. Lined with cobblestones and surrounded by historic brick buildings, this secluded spot offers a picturesque setting, making it a delightful discovery for those seeking a quiet escape from the city's bustle.

Theodore Parker Church – West Roxbury

Theodore Parker Unitarian Universalist Church is a historic church on Centre Street in West Roxbury. Built in 1900, the church is an example of Normanesque architecture designed by local architect Henry M. Seaver. The pink granite structure features a large gabled roof, a square tower with a belfry, and beautiful stained glass windows created by Louis Comfort Tiffany and his firm. The congregation that occupies the church has a rich history dating back to 1712. It was named after Theodore Parker, an influential Transcendentalist and abolitionist who served as the congregation's minister in the 1840s. The church's journey to its current location involved several transitions, including a split in the congregation and a fire that destroyed an earlier meetinghouse in 1890.In 1962, the church merged with another congregation and adopted the name Theodore Parker Unitarian Church. The building was recognized by the Boston Landmarks Commission in 1985 and is listed on the National Register of Historic Places. Today the church continues to serve as a Unitarian Universalist congregation and welcomes people from diverse backgrounds and beliefs.

The Loring-Greenough House – Jamaica Plain

The Loring-Greenough House holds significant historical and archi-tectural importance. Built in 1760, it stands as the last surviving 18th-century residence in the Sumner Hill area of Jamaica Plain. The house exemplifies high-style Georgian architecture, featuring a hip-roofed cube design with classical detailing. Originally constructed as a country estate for Commodore Joshua Loring, a British naval officer, the house played a role in the American Revolution. After Loring, a Loyalist, fled in 1774, the property was confiscated by colonial forces. It briefly served as a headquarters for General Nathanael Greene and later as a hospital for Continental Army soldiers following the Battle of Bunker Hill. The house's historical significance extends beyond the Revolutionary period. It was home to five generations of the Greenough family from 1784 to 1924, witnessing the transformation of Jamaica Plain from a rural area to a suburban neighborhood.

In 1924, facing the threat of demolition, the Jamaica Plain Tuesday Club purchased the house and grounds, preserving this important piece of local history. Today, the Loring-Greenough House serves as a mu-seum and community center, offering tours and hosting various events. It stands as a tangible link to Jamaica Plain's colonial past and subsequent development. The property's preservation allows visitors to experience an authentic 18th-century residence and provides valuable insights into the area's social, architectural, and cultural evolution over more than two centuries.

The Arnold Arboretum – Jamaica Plain/Roslindale

The Arnold Arboretum is a renowned botanical research institution and a free public park that spans 281 acres. Established in 1872, it is part of Harvard University and serves as a living museum dedicated to the study and appreciation of woody plants. The arboretum is notable for its extensive collection of over 15,000 trees, shrubs, and vines, including significant varieties such as Oriental cherries, lilacs, and magnolias, representing more than 6,000 different types of woody plants from around the world. Designed by landscape architects Frederick Law Olmsted and Charles Sprague Sargent, the arboretum's layout emphasizes a natural aesthetic, providing visitors with scenic views and educational opportunities. It is also a vital research center, housing an herbarium with over 1.3 million specimens and supporting ongoing botanical studies. The Arnold Arboretum is integrated into, enhancing urban green space and promoting biodiversity. It is a gem that has gems within it. One is Peter's Hill that offers panoramic views of the city skyline. This less-visited spot within the arboretum provides a peaceful escape with walking trails and benches for contemplation. The hill's elevation offers a unique vantage point.

The Shirley-Eustis House - Roxbury

The Shirley-Eustis House is a significant historical landmark built in 1747. It is one of the last remaining colonial governor's mansions in the original 13 American colonies. The house was originally constructed for William Shirley, the colonial governor of Massachusetts, and later became the home of William Eustis, another Massachusetts governor. This grand Georgian-style mansion was designed by Peter Harrison, considered the first colonial American architect. The property has undergone several changes over the centuries, including being moved to accommodate urban development and converted into apartments at one point. Recently, the Shirley-Eustis House Association acquired a nearby structure at 42-44 Shirley Street, believed to be a former stable house and living quarters for enslaved people. This acquisition has expanded the historical significance of the site, potentially making it one of only two surviving slave quarters in the northeastern United States.

The Shirley-Eustis House now serves as a museum, offering public tours and educational programs that explore various aspects of colonial and early American history, including the impact of the British Empire and the institution of slavery. The site continues to be a valuable resource for understanding Boston's complex past and the lives of both the elite and the enslaved during the 18th and early 19th centuries.

Castle Island – South Boston

Castle Island is a historically rich peninsula that offers a blend of recreation and scenic beauty. Originally an island until it was connected to the mainland in 1928, Castle Island is now a popular state park encompassing 22 acres along the shores of Boston Harbor. The site is home to Fort Independence, a significant military fortification constructed between 1834 and 1851, which has played a crucial role in various historical events, including the Revolutionary War. Edgar Allan Poe even served there as a soldier, and local lore suggests that his story "The Cask of Amontillado" was inspired by events at the fort. Visitors to Castle Island can enjoy a variety of activities, including walking or jogging along the scenic paths that offer stunning views of the harbor and the city skyline. The area features a beach at Pleasure Bay, which is ideal for swimming and sunbathing during the summer months. Additionally, families can take advantage of the playground and picnic areas scattered throughout the park. With its combination of history, natural beauty, and recreational opportunities, Castle Island remains a cherished destination for both locals and tourists alike.

The Fenway Victory Gardens – The Fenway

The Fenway Victory Gardens in Boston is a historic and thriving community garden with a rich legacy dating back to World War II. Established in 1942 during the Roosevelt Administration, it is the oldest continuously operating victory garden in the United States. Located within Frederick Law Olmsted's famous Emerald Necklace park system, the Fenway Victory Gardens spans 7.5 acres along Boston's Muddy

River. The gardens were part of a nationwide effort to combat food shortages during wartime, with victory gardens across the country producing nearly 40% of the nation's vegetable and fruit supply during World War II. Today, the Fenway Victory Gardens consists of over 500 individual plots tended by more than 375 community members from all Boston neighborhoods. These gardens reflect the city's diversity and cultural richness, featuring a variety of flowers, vegetables, herbs, and even some fish ponds and aviaries. The gardens serve multiple purposes beyond food production. They function as a public park, offering spaces for picnics, workshops, and wildlife observation. The Fenway Garden Society, established in 1944, oversees the gardens and organizes community events like FensFest, an annual harvest celebration. Despite its urban setting, the Fenway Victory Gardens provide a unique green space in the heart of Boston. Located near Fenway Park and surrounded by apartments, colleges, and hotels, it offers city residents a chance to connect with nature and participate in a living piece of American history.

Herter Park Amphitheater – Allston

Herter Park Amphitheater, located in Christian A. Herter Park along the Charles River in Allston, is a charming outdoor venue that accommodates 350 seated guests and an additional 200 on the lawn. This amphitheater has a rich history, having served as a cultural hub for over 60 years. Originally part of the Metropolitan Boston Arts Center, it hosted the Publick Theatre for 38 years until its decline in the late 2000s due to disrepair and financial difficulties. In recent years, efforts have been made to revitalize the amphitheater. A nonprofit organization, Friends of Herter Park, has been instrumental in restoring the venue, raising funds, and scheduling performances to bring arts back to the community. The amphitheater is now a welcoming space for all ages, offering free performances and a dog-friendly environment, encouraging visitors to pack a picnic and enjoy shows under the stars. The park itself is the largest section of open space in the Charles River Basin, featuring a community garden, playground, and ample recreational opportunities. It serves as a gathering place for various activities, including picnicking, kayaking, and sports.

North Square – North End

North Square is a historically rich area that has been a focal point of community life since the 17th century. Originally known as Clark's Square, it was anchored by the Old North Meeting House, where influential figures such as Increase Mather resided. The square is notably home to the Paul Revere House, built in 1680, which showcases the architectural styles of its time and connects visitors to the history of the American Revolution. In 1961, North Square was listed on the National Register of Historic Places, marking its significance in Boston's urban landscape. Recent restoration efforts have transformed it into a pedestrian-friendly space, enhancing its role as a gathering place. The project included the installation of public art pieces that reflect the area's maritime history and cultural heritage, making it a vibrant part of the Freedom Trail. Today, North Square serves as a testament to Boston's past, blending historical significance with modern initiatives. It remains a popular destination for both locals and tourists, offering a glimpse into the city's rich Italian heritage and community spirit.

SoWa Art + Design District – South End

The SoWa Art + Design District, short for "South of Washington," is a vibrant cultural enclave. This area has transformed from a collection of neglected industrial warehouses into a dynamic hub for artists, designers, and food enthusiasts. It features over 200 art studios, galleries, boutiques, and restaurants, making it a premier destination for creative expression and unique shopping experiences. One of the highlights of SoWa is the SoWa Open Market, held every Sunday from May to October. This market attracts artisans, farmers, and local vendors, showcasing handmade goods, fresh produce, and culinary delights. The neighborhood also hosts "SoWa First Fridays," where galleries and studios open their doors to the public, allowing visitors to engage with local artists and their work. SoWa is not just about art; it also offers a diverse culinary scene, with award-winning restaurants and cafes that provide a range of dining options. The area is characterized by its industrial-chic aesthetic, with many businesses housed in beautifully renovated warehouse spaces.

The district's revitalization began in the early 2000s, driven by developers like GTI Properties, which recognized the potential of the area. Today, SoWa stands as a testament to the power of creativity and community, making it an essential part of Boston's cultural landscape, where residents and visitors alike can live, work, shop, and enjoy a rich array of artistic and culinary experiences.

Franklin Park Zoo – Dorchester

Franklin Park Zoo is a 72-acre facility nestled within Boston's historic Franklin Park, the largest park in the city. Opened on October 4, 1912, the zoo is operated by Zoo New England and features a diverse range of animal exhibits, including red pandas, wallabies, and various species of birds and mammals. The zoo's design reflects a commitment to creating naturalistic habitats, with notable areas such as the African Tropical Forest and the Tropical Rainforest, which house exotic animals in settings that mimic their native environments. Franklin Park Zoo is particularly family-friendly, offering a large playground and interactive experiences, making it a popular destination for local families and visitors alike. Throughout its history, the zoo has undergone significant renovations and expansions, especially under the management of the Metropolitan District Commission and later Zoo New England. It has been accredited by the Association of Zoos and Aquariums since 1990, ensuring that it meets high standards for animal care and conservation. Visitors can enjoy various activities, including educational programs and seasonal events, enhancing the overall experience. Despite its smaller size compared to larger zoos, Franklin Park Zoo provides an engaging and accessible environment for animal lovers of all ages, contributing to the cultural and recreational landscape of Boston.

Chestnut Hill Reservation – Brighton

Chestnut Hill Reservation is a historic public recreation area. Established in the late 1860s, it encompasses approximately 120 acres, including the 85-acre Chestnut Hill Reservoir. The reservoir was originally part of Boston's water supply system, designed by Frederick Law Olmsted's son, and features a 1.5-mile circular path that offers scenic views of the Back Bay skyline and surrounding landscapes. The Reservation is recognized as a City of Boston Landmark and is listed on the National Register of Historic Places. It includes several historical structures, such as three gatehouses and pump houses, which exemplify 19th-century engineering and landscape design. Although the reservoir is no longer used for drinking water, it remains a popular destination for various recreational activities, including walking, jogging, birdwatching, and fishing. The Reilly Memorial Recreation Center, situated nearby, provides facilities for swimming and ice skating, enhancing the area's appeal as a community hub. The Chestnut Hill Reservation continues to serve as a vital green space for both residents and visitors, reflecting its historical significance and ongoing recreational value.

Beantown

Though it's also known as the Cradle of Liberty and even the Hub of the Universe by some, no nickname has stuck to Boston quite like Beantown. On one level, the origin is as simple as you'd expect: Boston baked beans are a regional dish differentiated by the use of molasses for a bit of sweetness alongside the salt pork and/or bacon flavoring. There's also more history to it, as the tradition dates back to the 17th century and involves both Native Americans (who made baked beans without the molasses) and the slave trade (which is how the area got much of its molasses in the first place).

For quite a long time - even through today, to an extent - Beantown was used more by sailors and other visitors than by actual locals. Some nicknames aren't quite as beloved by locals as they are by the rest of us.

Boston's Best Walking Trails

Charles River Esplanade: This scenic trail along the Charles River offers beautiful views of the water and the city skyline. It's perfect for a leisurely stroll or a jog, seamlessly blending natural beauty with urban charm. Stretching alongside the iconic Charles River, this scenic esplanade offers a vibrant mix of recreational spaces, walking and biking paths, and lush greenery. With breathtaking views of the river and the city skyline, the Esplanade provides a tranquil escape from the bustling city life. Its well-maintained trails invite joggers, cyclists, and strollers to enjoy the serenity of the water, while strategically placed benches and parks offer perfect spots for relaxation. The Charles River Esplanade is not only a haven for outdoor enthusiasts but also a cultural hub, hosting events and festivities that celebrate the rich heritage of the Charles River and its surroundings.

Boston Common and Public Garden: These historic parks in the heart of the city offer picturesque paths surrounded by lush greenery and iconic monuments. Established in 1634, Boston Common is a historic haven, one of the nation's oldest public parks. It offers a vast expanse for leisure, hosting events and serving as a tranquil retreat. Adjacent to the Common, the Public Garden, dating back to 1837, enchants with meticulously manicured lawns, vibrant flower displays, and the iconic Swan Boats gliding across serene waters. These interconnected green spaces, steeped in colonial history, provide an oasis within the city, inviting residents and visitors to meander along scenic paths, appreciate statues and enjoy a timeless escape from the urban hustle. Boston Common and Public Garden stand as verdant gems, weaving nature seamlessly into the city's tapestry.

Freedom Trail: This 2.5-mile-long trail takes you through some of Boston's most historic sites, including the Massachusetts State House, Paul Revere's House, and the USS Constitution. Starting at Boston Common, stroll past the Massachusetts State House, where independence sentiments simmered. Peek into the Granary Burying Ground, where figures like Sam Adams and John Hancock rest. Visit Faneuil Hall, a "cradle of liberty" for fiery speeches and political gatherings. Follow the red brick line past landmarks like the Old North Church, famous for its "one if by land, two if by sea" lantern signal. Stand beneath the gilded dome of the State House and imagine fiery debates. Immerse yourself in the past at sites like the Old South Meeting House, a hub for resistance, and the Paul Revere House, a preserved 17th-century home. Each stop whispers stories of revolution, resistance, and the fight for freedom. The Freedom Trail isn't just a walk; it's a time capsule, transporting you to the heart of American history in mere steps.

Castle Island Loop: Located in South Boston, this waterfront trail offers stunning views of Boston Harbor and passes by Fort Independence. This scenic loop surrounds Castle Island, featuring a well-maintained pathway along the shoreline, offering stunning views of Boston Harbor and the city skyline. The highlight of the loop is the historic Fort Independence, a military fortress dating back to the Revolutionary War era, providing a glimpse into the region's rich heritage. Visitors can enjoy a leisurely walk, jog, or bike ride along the waterfront, taking in the salty sea breeze and watching boats sail by. The loop is a popular destination for locals and tourists alike, providing a serene escape with its coastal charm and historical significance, making Castle Island Loop a cherished gem in Boston's recreational landscape.

Arnold Arboretum: Part of the Emerald Necklace, this 281-acre botanical garden in Jamaica Plain features a variety of trees, shrubs, and plants from around the world. Established in 1872, this living museum is managed by Harvard University and is a haven for plant enthusiasts and nature lovers alike. Designed by renowned landscape architect Frederick Law Olmsted, the arboretum boasts a diverse collection of woody plants, including rare and endangered species, displayed in thematic gardens and naturalistic settings. Visitors can explore winding paths, serene

148

meadows, and the Hunnewell Building's educational facilities. The Arboretum not only serves as a research hub for plant science but also provides a tranquil escape, inviting contemplation and appreciation for the wonders of the plant kingdom within the heart of Boston.

Jamaica Pond Loop: This 1.5-mile loop around Jamaica Pond in Jamaica Plain offers tranquil views of the water and is surrounded by walking paths and picnic areas. Encircled by tree-lined paths, the loop provides a popular destination for walkers, joggers, and cyclists, allowing them to enjoy the tranquil waters, lush greenery, and diverse birdlife. The path offers glimpses of Boston's skyline and historic homes, creating a harmonious blend of urban and natural landscapes. With amenities such as benches, picnic areas, and the iconic boathouse, Jamaica Pond Loop invites locals and visitors to unwind, exercise, and appreciate the idyllic surroundings. The loop's accessibility and scenic charm make it a cherished destination for those seeking a peaceful escape within the vibrant city.

Harborwalk: Stretching along Boston's waterfront, the Harborwalk offers a variety of walking paths, parks, and public art installations. The nearly 40-mile public waterfront walkway winds through Boston's waterfront neighborhoods, stretching from Chelsea Creek to the Neponset River, through East Boston, Charlestown, North End, Downtown, Fort Point, South Boston and Dorchester. It is designed to connect the public to Boston Harbor and link the water's edge to the city's open space network. Start in bustling Downtown, where skyscrapers kiss the sky. Pass the iconic New England Aquarium and Long Wharf, remnants of Boston's maritime past. In the North End, savor Italian delicacies while gazing at charming fishing boats. South Boston beckons with vibrant parks like Castle Island, perfect for picnics and kite flying. Continue to Dorchester, where the Harborwalk transforms into a peaceful escape, offering stunning sunset views over the water. The journey isn't just about sights; it's about experiencing Boston's unique connection to its harbor. Hop on a ferry, kayak alongside the path, or simply soak in the atmosphere at waterfront restaurants.

Southwest Corridor Park: This linear park runs along a former railroad corridor and features walking and biking paths, playgrounds, and community gardens - spanning from Boston's Back Bay to the neighborhoods of Jamaica Plain and Roxbury. Once a railroad corridor, this linear park now offers a diverse range of recreational opportunities and community spaces. The park features tree-lined pathways, vibrant gardens, playgrounds, and sports facilities, providing a haven for cyclists, joggers, and families alike. Dotted with public art installations and seating areas, it fosters a sense of community engagement and cultural expression. Southwest Corridor Park serves as a model for sustainable urban planning, seamlessly integrating greenery into the cityscape, and connecting neighborhoods. Its role as a dynamic public space contributes to the well-being of residents while preserving a rich historical legacy, making it a beloved and vibrant asset in the heart of Massachusetts.

Boston Harbor Islands: Accessible by ferry, the Boston Harbor Islands offer a range of walking trails and outdoor recreational activities, including camping and birdwatching. The scenic archipelago comprises 34 islands and peninsulas within reach of Boston's bustling waterfront, creating a coastal paradise. Rich in history, these islands offer a unique blend of natural beauty and cultural significance. Accessible by ferry, the islands feature diverse landscapes, from sandy beaches to lush forests. Spectacle Island, with its panoramic views, and George's Island, home to the historic Fort Warren, stand out as popular destinations. Visitors can explore hiking trails, engage in birdwatching, or simply enjoy the maritime scenery. The Boston Harbor Islands serve as a recreational haven, preserving ecosystems, historic sites, and providing a refreshing escape from the urban landscape, making them an integral part of the region's maritime and natural heritage.

Stony Brook Reservation: Stony Brook Reservation is a 475-acre urban oasis that offers a peaceful retreat within the city's bounds. The reservation is primarily in Hyde Park, with smaller sections in Roslindale and West Roxbury. Established in the early 20th century, this reservation is characterized by a diverse landscape, featuring woodlands, meadows, and the meandering Stony Brook. The park provides an array of recrea-

150

tional opportunities, including hiking trails, picnic areas, and a swimming pool during the summer months. Stony Brook Reservation is also a haven for birdwatchers and nature enthusiasts, with its varied habitats supporting a rich biodiversity. Its commitment to conservation, combined with accessible outdoor amenities, makes it a beloved destination for locals seeking solace in nature and a testament to the importance of preserving green spaces within urban environments.

Neponset River Greenway: This multi-use trail follows the Neponset River through several Boston neighborhoods, offering beautiful views of the river and surrounding wildlife. Its 13-mile path weaves through diverse landscapes alongside the scenic Neponset River. Imagine cycling beneath a canopy of trees, feeling the cool river breeze, and spotting hidden wildlife.

Starting in Dorchester, explore Pope John Paul II Park, perfect for picnicking, before hopping on the paved trail. Immerse yourself in bustling neighborhoods like Milton, passing vibrant murals and charming cafes. Cross the iconic Harvest River Bridge, a modern marvel offering breathtaking river views. Further along, discover hidden gems like the secluded Tenean Beach, ideal for relaxing or kayaking. Explore the Neponset River Reservation, a haven for birdwatchers, with marshes, meadows, and tranquil trails. The trail seamlessly connects with parks like Ronan Park, offering stunning vistas of the Boston skyline.

Whether you're an avid cyclist, a casual walker, or simply seeking nature's escape, the Neponset River Greenway offers a unique experience. It's a chance to rediscover Boston's natural beauty, one peaceful pedal stroke or mindful step at a time.

Franklin Park: This expansive park in Roxbury features walking trails, picnic areas, and the Franklin Park Zoo. Sprawling over 700 acres, Franklin Park is a green oasis offering something for everyone. Imagine rolling hills perfect for picnicking, tranquil woodlands ideal for nature walks, and even a zoo buzzing with exotic animals. Start at the Arnold Arboretum, a 265-acre wonderland containing over 15,000 trees and shrubs from around the world, and wander through vibrant spring blooms or witness autumn's fiery foliage transformation. In the heart of the park,

Franklin Park Zoo houses animals, including lion, giraffes and gorillas that mesmerize children and adults alike.

For sports enthusiasts, the park boasts tennis courts, a golf course, and even a running track. The iconic Playstead, a vast green space, hosts soccer games, festivals, and concerts, drawing crowds throughout the year. Explore hidden gems like the Stone Flower, a Japanese-inspired garden, or simply relax by the serene Echo Lake.

Whether seeking recreation, adventure, or a quiet escape, Franklin Park offers an unparalleled experience. It's a vibrant tapestry of nature, history, and community, making it a true Boston gem.

Trivia Questions

Answers on page 155

1. What is Boston's official nickname?

2. What is the largest park in Boston?

3. What is the oldest public park in the United States?

4. What is the tallest building in Boston?

5. When was Boston founded?

6. What is the official state drink of Massachusetts?

7. How long is the Freedom Trail?

8. What is the name of the historic Boston hotel that played a key role in the American Revolution?

9. What is the name of the Boston Red Sox home ballpark?

10. What was Boston's original name?

11. What river runs through Boston?

12. What is the name of Boston's basketball team?

13. What is the name of the famous Boston cream pie bakery?

14. What is the oldest public school in the United States?

15. What is the name of the famous Boston tea party ship?

16. Who founded the Massachusetts Bay Colony, which eventually became Boston?

17. Who was the first female governor of Massachusetts and the United States?

18. What is the name of the famous Boston-born culinary superstar?

19. Who wrote the famous novel "The Scarlet Letter," which is set in Boston?

20. What famous university had its first campus in Boston?

21. What is the name of the famous marathon in Boston?

22. What is the name of the Boston-based news outlet that broke the Watergate scandal?

23. What is the name of the famous outdoor shopping center in Boston?

24. What is the name of the famous Boston-based sportswriter?

25. What dessert was made famous in Boston?

26. What was the first permanent medical facility in Boston?

27. What is the biggest football stadium in Boston?

28. Who is the current mayor of Boston?

29. What baseball teams played in the city series in the 1950s?

30. Who invented the telephone and was born in Boston?

31. Name of the famous Boston-based brewery?

32. Name of the famous Boston-based seafood restaurant?

33. Where is there a duplicate set of "Make Way for Ducklings"?

34. Where was John F. Kennedy's apartment located in Boston?

35. What is the name of the famous Boston-based bakery that makes cannoli?

Trivia Answers

1. The Cradle of Liberty
2. Franklin Park
3. Boston Common
4. The John Hancock Tower
5. 1630
6. Cranberry juice
7. 2.5 miles
8. The Omni Parker House
9. Fenway Park
10. Shawmut
11. The Charles River
12. The Boston Celtics
13. Parker's Restaurant in the Parker House
14. Boston Latin School
15. The Beaver
16. John Winthrop
17. Jane Swift
18. Julia Child
19. Nathaniel Hawthorne
20. Boston College
21. The Boston Marathon
22. The Boston Globe
23. Faneuil Hall Marketplace
24. Bob Ryan
25. Boston Cream Pie
26. The Boston Dispensary (1796)
27. Harvard Stadium
28. Mayor Michelle Wu
29. Boston Red Sox and Boston Braves
30. Alexander Graham Bell
31. Samuel Adams
32. Legal Sea Foods
33. Moscow, Russia
34. Bowdoin Street on Beacon Hill
35. Mike's Pastry

Photo Answers

1. The Embrace statue is located on Boston Common. It commemorates the embrace of Martin Luther King, Jr. and his wife Coretta Scott King.

2. It memorializes Robert Gold Shaw and the Massachusetts 54th Regiment that was one of the first black Union Army units to participate in the Civil War. It is located on the Beacon Street side of Boston Common.

3. James Michael Curley, who served four terms as Mayor of Boston.

4. Boston's Old City Hall, one of the first examples of Second Empire architecture in the United States was used as city hall from 1865 to 1969.

5. The statue, one of the largest bronze statues in Boston, depicts President George Washington riding a horse. The height of the statue and pedestal is 38 feet tall and has stood at the Commonwealth Avenue entrance to the Boston Public Garden since 1869.

6. The Old Corner Bookstore, Downtown Boston's oldest commercial building and home to 19th century publishing giant Ticknor and Fields, is at the corner of School and Washington streets, near Downtown Crossing.

7. The Donald McKay memorial in East Boston, features a pavilion at Piers Park, honoring McKay's legacy as a renowned ship-builder of clipper ships, including the famous "Flying Cloud."

8. Fort Independence, formerly known as Castle William, sits on top of Castle Island in South Boston. With a strategic location on Boston Harbor, this site has served as the home to military forti-fications for hundreds of years. The Castle Island Association provides free guided and self-guided tours of the fort.

9. A Three Family or Triple Decker.

10. White Stadium, formally the George R. White Memorial Sta-dium, is a 10,519-seat facility located in Boston's Franklin Park that was constructed between 1947 and 1949 for the use of Bos-ton Public Schools athletes.

11. The Exchange is located at the end of the Fish Pier off Northern Avenue on Boston's Waterfront. It once housed New England's oldest daily fish auction, and now is a state-of-the-art conference center.

12. The building did not move but the land was filled so it was no longer on the waterfront.

13. It was located in what is now known as Columbia Point – or Har-bor Point - in Dorchester and its occupants were Italian soldiers who were captured during World War II.

14. Alumni Stadium and other Boston College facilities.

15. The First Church in Roxbury, also known as the First Church of Roxbury, is the current headquarters of the Unitarian Universalist Urban Ministry. A church on this site has been in use since 1632 when early English settlers built the first meetinghouse.

16. Tapes from conversations that President Kennedy had recorded unbeknownst to the other person in the conversation. They are available to the public.

City Seal

The City Seal was adopted in 1823, and the first image of the seal was published in 1827. It became the official seal in 1914. The City Seal is a circular image that features:

- A view of the City of Boston

- The motto, "SICUT PATRIBUS, SIT DEUS NOBIS" (which means, "God be with us as he was with our fathers")

- The inscription, "BOSTONIA CONDITA AD. 1630 CIVITATIS REGIMINE DONATA AD. 1822" (which means, "City-Status Granted by the Authority of the State in 1822")